HIKING THE OVERLAND TRACK

TASMANIA: CRADLE MOUNTAIN–LAKE ST CLAIR NATIONAL PARK

by Warwick Sprawson

JUNIPER HOUSE, MURLEY MOSS,
OXENHOLME ROAD, KENDAL, CUMBRIA LA9 7RL
www.cicerone.co.uk

First edition 2020
ISBN: 978 1 78631 013 2
Printed in China on behalf of Latitude Press Ltd
A catalogue record for this book is available from the British Library.

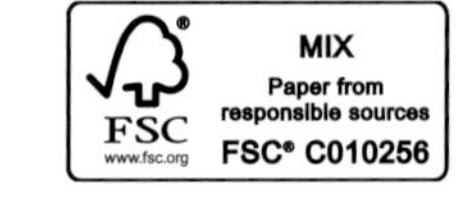

Route mapping by Lovell Johns www.lovelljohns.com
All photographs are by the author unless otherwise stated.
Contains OpenStreetMap.org data © OpenStreetMap contributors, CC-BY-SA. NASA relief data courtesy of ESRI

Acknowledgements

First and foremost, thanks to Yasmin Kelsall for saying 'Yes' on top of Mt Oakleigh. Let's keep adventuring together.

Sincere thanks to the excellent photographers who generously allowed the use of their photos in this book, particularly Dave Watts (www.davewattsphoto.com) for the mammals, Alan Fletcher for the birds and Michael Thow for the snakes. Thanks also to Karen McGregor for her GPS wizardry and the Tasmania Parks and Wildlife Service for their fact-checking help.

Updates to this Guide

While every effort is made by our authors to ensure the accuracy of guidebooks as they go to print, changes can occur during the lifetime of an edition. Any updates that we know of for this guide will be on the Cicerone website (www.cicerone.co.uk/1013/updates), so please check before planning your trip. We also advise that you check information about such things as transport, accommodation and shops locally.

The route maps in this guide are derived from publicly available data, databases and crowd-sourced data. As such they have not been through the detailed checking procedures that would generally be applied to a published map from an official mapping agency, although naturally we have reviewed them closely in the light of local knowledge as part of the preparation of this guide.

We are always grateful for information about any discrepancies between a guidebook and the facts on the ground, sent by email to updates@cicerone.co.uk or by post to Cicerone, Juniper House, Murley Moss, Oxenholme Road, Kendal, LA9 7RL.

Register your book: to sign up to receive free updates, special offers and GPX files where available, register your book at www.cicerone.co.uk.

CONTENTS

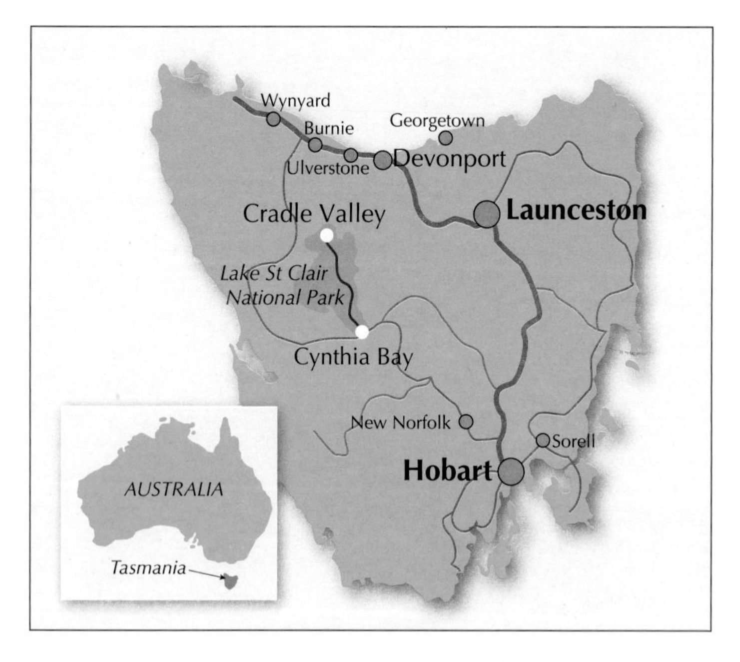

Front cover: A mountain tarn near the summit of Mt Ossa (Stage 4 sidetrip)

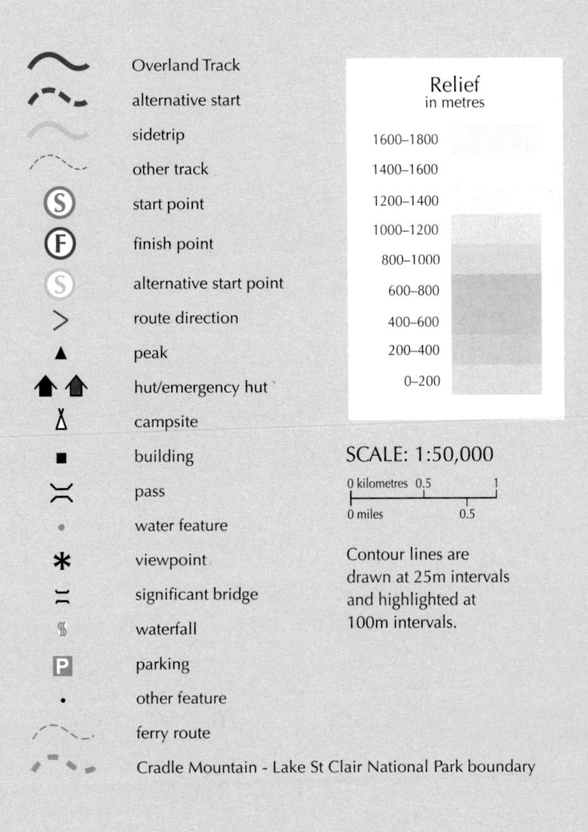

GPX files for all routes can be downloaded free at www.cicerone.co.uk/1013/GPX.

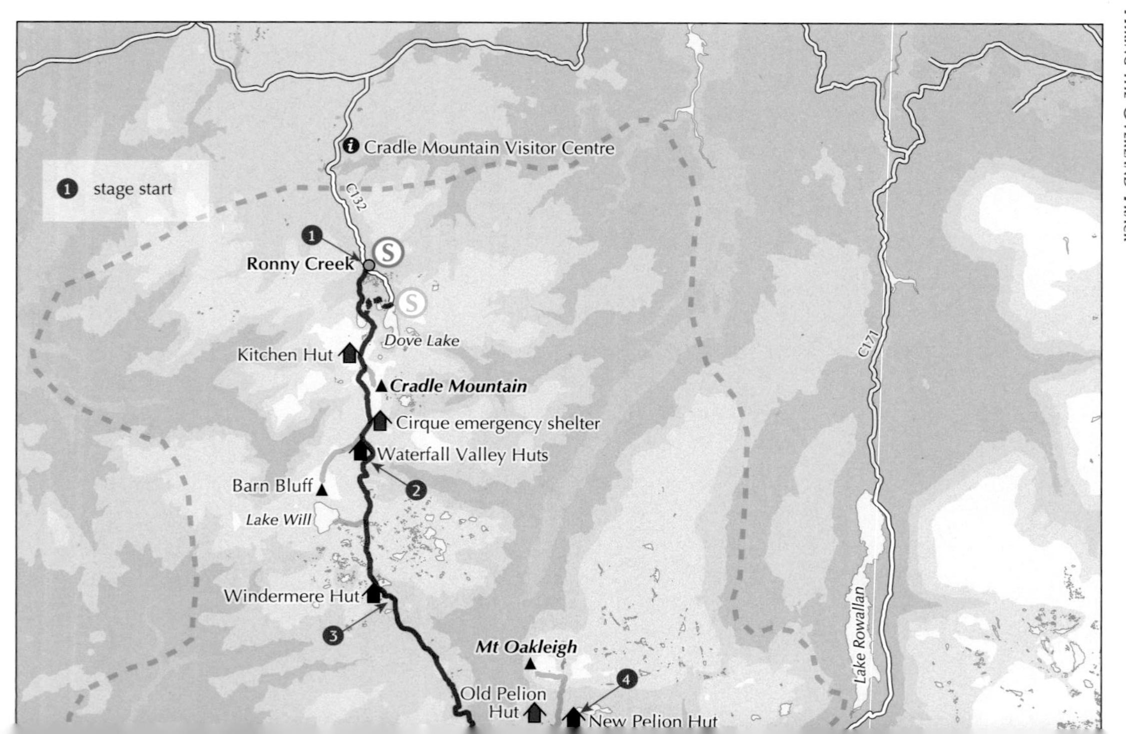
stage start
Cradle Mountain Visitor Centre
C132
Ronny Creek
Dove Lake
Kitchen Hut
Cradle Mountain
Cirque emergency shelter
Waterfall Valley Huts
Barn Bluff
Lake Will
Windermere Hut
Mt Oakleigh
Old Pelion Hut
New Pelion Hut
C171
Lake Rowallan

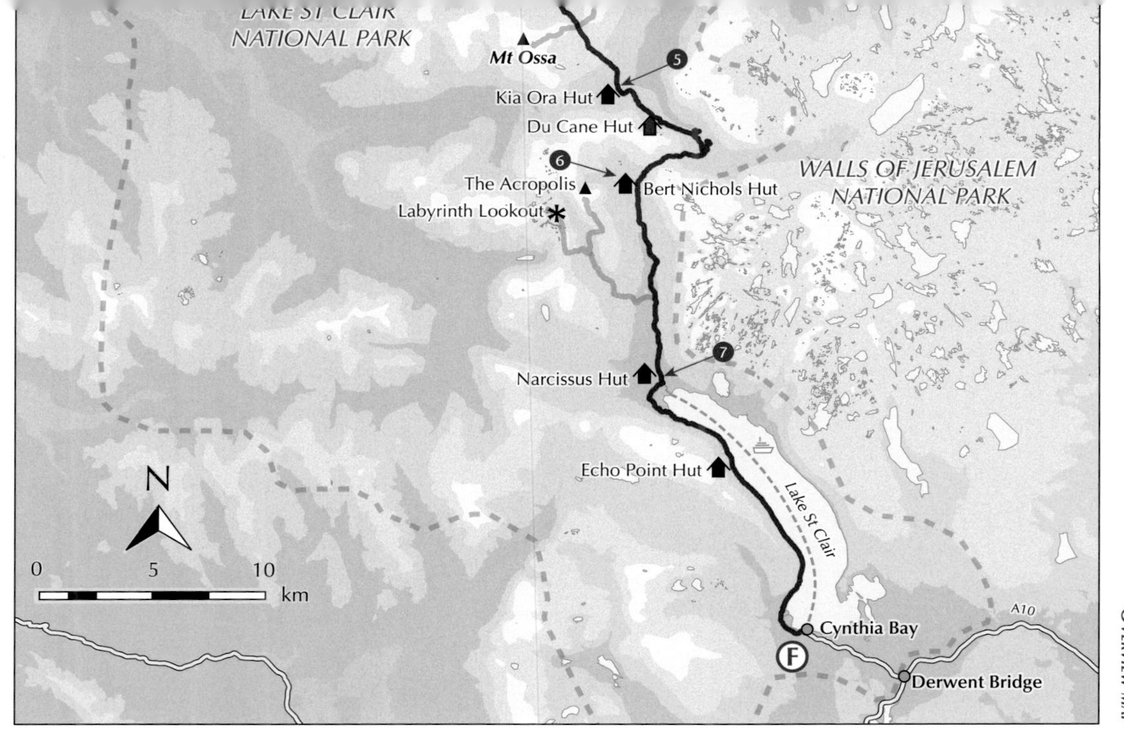
NATIONAL PARK
Mt Ossa
Kia Ora Hut
Du Cane Hut
The Acropolis
Bert Nichols Hut
Labyrinth Lookout
WALLS OF JERUSALEM
NATIONAL PARK
Narcissus Hut
Echo Point Hut
Lake St Clair
Cynthia Bay
Derwent Bridge
A10
F
5
6
7
N
0
5
10
km

Mountain safety

Every mountain walk has its dangers, and those described in this guidebook are no exception. All who walk or climb in the mountains should recognise this and take responsibility for themselves and their companions along the way. The author and publisher have made every effort to ensure that the information contained in this guide was correct when it went to press, but, except for any liability that cannot be excluded by law, they cannot accept responsibility for any loss, injury or inconvenience sustained by any person using this book.

Distress signal *(emergency only)*
In Tasmania any pattern of 3 is a distress signal, such as 3 whistle blasts, 3 torch or mirror flashes, or 3 lines tramped in the snow.

Helicopter rescue
The following signals are used to communicate with a helicopter:

Help needed: raise both arms above head to form a 'Y'

Help not needed: raise one arm above head, extend other arm downward

Emergency telephone numbers
In an emergency dial 000.

Weather reports
Bureau of Meteorology: www.bom.gov.au

Mountain rescue can be very expensive – be adequately insured.

Pinestone Valley on the way to Kia Ora Hut (Stage 4)

ROUTE SUMMARY TABLES

MAIN ROUTE

Stage		Time (hr)	Distance (km)	Ascent/ descent (m)	Grade
Stage 1	Ronny Creek (Cradle Valley) to Waterfall Valley Huts	3½–5½	11.0	565/405	Medium–hard
Stage 2	Waterfall Valley Huts to Windermere Hut	2–3	7.7	200/230	Easy–medium
Stage 3	Windermere Hut to New Pelion Hut	5–6½	15.3	520/665	Medium
Stage 4	New Pelion Hut to Kia Ora Hut	3½–4	8.6	335/335	Medium
Stage 5	Kia Ora Hut to Bert Nichols Hut	3½–4½	9.8	380/350	Medium
Stage 6	Bert Nichols Hut to Narcissus Hut	2¾–3¾	10.1	165/310	Easy
Stage 7	Narcissus Hut to Cynthia Bay	5–7	17.2	710/710	Easy–medium
Total		7 days	79.7	2875/3005	

SIDETRIPS OFF MAIN TRACK

Stage	Sidetrip	Time (return)	Distance (return)	Total ascent/ descent (return, m)	Grade
Stage 1	Cradle Mountain	2½–3½hr	2.6km	355	Medium–hard
Stage 1	Barn Bluff	3–4hr	6.2km	480	Medium–hard
Stage 2	Lake Will Beach	1¼hr	3.2km	50	Easy
Stage 3	River Forth Lookout	10min	130m	10	Easy
Stage 3	Old Pelion Hut	30min	880m	30	Easy
Stage 3	Mt Oakleigh	5–6hr	9.2km	625	Medium
Stage 4	Mt Ossa	3½–4½hr	5.8km	605	Medium–hard
Stage 4	Mt Pelion East	1½–2½hr	2.8km	290	Medium
Stage 5	D'Alton and Fergusson Falls	45min	1.7km	120	Easy–Medium
Stage 5	Hartnett Falls	1–1½hr	2.2km	85	Easy
Stage 6	Pine Valley Hut (an over-night trip is recommended)	1½–2hr (one way)	4.9km (one way)	150/100 (one way)	Easy

SIDETRIPS FROM PINE VALLEY HUT

Sidetrip	Time (return)	Distance (return)	Total ascent/ descent, (return, m)	Grade
The Labyrinth Lookout	4–5hr	7.2km	560	Medium–hard
The Acropolis	5–6hr	8.2km	840	Hard

Wombat Pool. Keep it clean, you might be the one drinking it (Stage 1 alternative start, photo: François Maréchal)

THE OVERLAND HUTS

Hut	Distance from previous overnight hut (km)	Distance from Ronny Creek start (km)	Number of bunks	Heating	Water source
Start: Ronny Creek (Cradle Valley)	0.0	0.0	-	-	-
Kitchen Hut	*5.5*	*5.5*	*Emergency only*	*No*	*No source*
Scott-Kilvert Memorial Hut (2.1 km off main track)	(10.6)	(10.6)	20	Yes	Tank
Cirque Emergency Shelter	*8.5*	*8.5*	*Emergency only*	*No*	*No source*
Waterfall Valley Huts	11.0	11.0	24 (plus 4 in old hut)*	Yes	Tank
Windermere Hut	7.7	18.7	16	Yes	Tank
Old Pelion Hut (440m off main track)	*(14.8)*	*(33.5)*	*Emergency only*	*No*	*Creek*
New Pelion Hut	15.3	34.0	36	Yes	Tank
Kia Ora Hut	8.6	42.6	20	Yes	Tank
Du Cane Hut	*2.9*	*45.5*	*Emergency only*	*No*	*No source*
Bert Nichols Hut	9.8	52.4	24	Yes	Tank
Pine Valley Hut (4.9km off main track)	(10.6)	(63.0)	24	Yes	Tank
Narcissus Hut	10.1	62.5	18	Yes	Tank
Echo Point Hut	6.5	69.0	8	Yes	Creek or lake
Finish: Cynthia Bay	17.2	79.7	-	-	-

* A new 34-person hut at Waterfall Valley is due for completion in May 2020

Du Cane Hut (Stage 5)

INTRODUCTION

According to a recent Tasmania Parks and Wildlife Service survey, 55 per cent of hikers rated the Overland Track as "one of the best things I have ever done in my life". Another 39 per cent rated it as "one of the best things I have done in the past 12 months", while, encouragingly, only 0.4 per cent opted for "glad it's over and I never want to go bushwalking again".

It's little wonder 'the Overland' garners such high praise. Nearly eighty kilometres of glacier-carved valleys, vast buttongrass moorlands, mossy rainforests, rugged peaks, thundering waterfalls, alpine meadows and peaceful lakes – the track teeming with plants and animals found nowhere else on earth. It's a different Australia to the one often portrayed; a landscape still raw from the last ice age, its history revealed in its unique plants, animals and geography. The Overland Track is one of the world's great walks.

While it's possible to walk from Cradle Valley to Lake St Clair (or vice versa) in just four or five days, allowing yourself a few more days, ideally eight or nine, gives you time for a rest day if the weather turns bad, and also time to explore some of the Overland's sidetrips. These tracks head off from the Overland's main spine and are the highlight for many walkers: from Pine Valley's ancient rainforests to the breathtaking views among the stone pinnacles of Mt Oakleigh.

Part of the reason the Overland Track has become so popular with hikers from around the world is its accessibility. The main track is well marked and maintained, with boardwalks above the boggiest ground, bridges over creeks and a network of basic huts, all of which make the track suitable for hikers of average fitness. Yet there are plenty of challenges for experienced hikers too, with steep sidetrips to mountain peaks – such as Mt Ossa, at 1617m Tasmania's highest peak – and into wilderness areas like The Labyrinth.

Despite its fame and popularity, hikers need to keep in mind that this is a remote area with frequent wild weather. To enjoy the walk – and not just endure it – you need to be well prepared. This book contains everything you'll need for your trip: advice on what to bring, how to get there, track notes, maps and historical information, plus information on the plants and animals you're likely to see along the way. So drag your pack out from the back of the cupboard and let's hike the Overland Track.

The view from near the top of Mt Oakleigh (Stage 3 sidetrip)

HIGHLIGHTS

Of course everyone will have their own highlights, but definite favourites include:

- The jagged profile of Cradle Mountain as seen across Dove Lake (alternative start, Stage 1).
- Scrambling up the lichen-spotted boulders to the summit of Cradle Mountain (sidetrip, Stage 1).
- The panorama from among the huge rock columns near the summit of Mt Oakleigh (sidetrip, Stage 3).
- Enjoying the sweeping view from the veranda of New Pelion Hut (Stages 3 and 4).
- Pine Valley Hut, deep in the heart of the rainforest, as well as its two lesser-known sidetrips: the spectacular peak of The Acropolis and the otherworldly landscape of The Labyrinth (sidetrip, Stage 6).
- The lovely, varied forest of the Narcissus Valley, particularly the southern end towards Narcissus Hut (Stage 6).
- The glorious, golden autumn foliage of the deciduous beech, often best around late April.

LOCATION

The Overland Track is located in Tasmania, an Australian island-state off the mainland's south-east coast. The island is wild and wonderful, with over 1.58 million hectares – 20 per cent of the state – protected within the Tasmanian World Heritage Area, including the 160,000 hectare Cradle Mountain–Lake St Clair National Park.

The Overland Track is in the Cradle Mountain–Lake St Clair National Park in central north-west Tasmania. Cradle Mountain, in the north of the park, is 85km from Devonport and 181km from Launceston. Lake St Clair, in the south, is 180km from both Hobart and Launceston. The location of the track is shown of the overview map at the start of the book.

Every year about 9000 people hike the track, either the entire 79.7km from Cradle Mountain to the south end of Lake St Clair, or an abbreviated 62.5km version, finishing at the top of Lake St Clair and catching a ferry across the lake instead of walking the final leg.

While the hike is said to be from Cradle Mountain to Lake St Clair, the hike actually starts in the Cradle Valley at Ronny Creek (about 5km north of the mountain) while the southern end terminates at Cynthia Bay (at the southern end of Lake St Clair). As discussed in the 'Hiking direction' section, out of peak season the track can also be walked in the opposite direction, from Lake St Clair to Cradle Mountain.

Cradle Mountain and Dove Lake (Stage 1 alternative start)

As well as the thousands of hikers who complete the Overland annually, tens of thousands more walk part of the track. Word of the area's beauty has made the national park an international destination, with 22 per cent of Overlanders now from overseas. It's this cosmopolitan mix of hikers, brought together by their appreciation of the Tasmanian wilderness, that helps elevate the Overland to its iconic status.

HISTORY

Aboriginal history

People have been living in Tasmania for at least 35,000 years. For 20,000 years Aboriginal Tasmanians were the southernmost people on Earth, exhibiting a remarkable resilience to ice age conditions. Within the Cradle Mountain–Lake St Clair National Park, a rock shelter on the Forth River, Parmerpar Meerthenar, was periodically occupied from 32,000BC right through to 1200AD. To put this timescale in context, within Aboriginal Tasmanian history it's only relatively recently that the land mass of Tasmania became an island: a mere 13,000 years since the ice age ended and flooded Bass Strait.

Archaeological evidence of Aboriginal occupation such as rock marking, artefacts, quarries and rock shelters have been found the length of the Overland Track. Aboriginal Tasmanians used well-marked tracks for hunting, gathering and trade. Fire was used regularly to open paths for travel, to hunt the animals driven out by the flames and to promote new plant growth (which in turn would attract more game). Some of the buttongrass moors along the track are likely the result of thousands of years of regular burning.

When white settlers first arrived in Tasmania (then called Van Diemen's Land) in 1803, the island's Aboriginal population was estimated to be between 3000 and 15,000, although many believe it was considerably higher. The Big River Tribe, whose territory the Overland is in, consisted of between 400 and 500 people. Theirs was a rich land with abundant hunting grounds around the lakes and river flats. Men used spears to hunt wallabies and wombats, while women harvested plants and climbed trees to catch possums. Despite the cold weather they wore few clothes, preferring to protect themselves against the elements with a mixture of fat, ochre and charcoal. The first explorers in the Lake St Clair area noted the Aboriginals' substantial dome-shaped huts, built with a framework of bent branches and thatched with grass and bark. These huts, arranged in small villages, were believed to have been occupied most of the year.

Soon European settlement began to encroach upon the tribes' territories, the settlers' sheep competing with game for food. While Aboriginal society was based on sharing and exchange, European culture was based on private ownership. When the Europeans saw no fences or farms they claimed the land, not understanding that the Aboriginals expected payment in the form of hunting dogs, tea, sugar and blankets. Conflict grew as more and more settlers arrived.

By the 1820s white settlers were rapidly overrunning the island with their sheep. With their traditional way of life under threat, Tasmanian Aboriginals began to fight back, raiding huts, stealing firearms, spearing stock and burning wheat, huts and homes. The colony was terrified, the settlers demanding the Aboriginals either be controlled or eliminated. In 1828 martial law was declared, allowing soldiers to arrest or shoot any Aboriginal found in the settled districts (the centre and south-east of the island). The minutes of the Executive Council said the aim was, "To inspire them with terror...the only effectual means of security for the future."

By one estimate, over 60 per cent of the total Aboriginal population died in the 12 months after martial law was declared, yet no white person was ever convicted of murder. In 1830 the government even offered a bounty for Aboriginal captives: five pounds per adult, two pounds per child, but the slaughter meant many more were killed than captured alive.

On 31 December 1831 the last of the Big River Tribe still on their land surrendered near Lake Echo, about 35km east of Lake St Clair. The 16 men, nine women and one child remaining were exhausted by the conflict and grieving for their dead and abducted.

Further north, Cradle Mountain became the last refuge of the final Aboriginal family to live a traditional lifestyle, the group managing to evade capture until 1842.

Across Tasmania 220 Aboriginal survivors were gathered up and sent to Wybalenna, a bleak settlement on Flinders Island in Bass Strait where the authorities hoped they would become Christian farmers. But away from their land, living in crowded houses in prison-like conditions and forbidden from practising their traditions, most soon succumbed to disease, poor diet and despair. Conditions were no better at Oyster Cove near Hobart where 47 survivors were moved in 1847.

Many Australians were taught that the last Tasmanian Aboriginal, Truganini, died in 1876 and that it took just 73 years to annihilate an ancient culture.

It's true that the devastation was so rapid that relatively little is known about these first Tasmanians. But despite war, dispossession and discrimination, Tasmanian Aboriginals survived, having escaped to the islands of Bass Strait to live with European sealers.

Today over 25,000 people identify as Indigenous in Tasmania, and are proudly recovering and renewing their culture. Indigenous people continue to visit the Cradle Mountain–Lake St Clair area to maintain the traditions of their ancestors.

Truganini, also known as 'Trugemanner' or 'Lalla Rooke' (Tasmanian Archive and Heritage Office)

European settlement

Joseph Fossey was the first European recorded in the Cradle Mountain area in 1827 as he surveyed the north-west of the island for grazing land on behalf of the Van Diemen's Land Company (VDL). Fossey returned to the Cradle region in 1828 when he is likely to have climbed Cradle Mountain to get a view over the surrounding country. He named the mountain from its resemblance to a cradle, although it's uncertain whether he meant a baby's cradle or a goldminer's. Henry Hellyer, another VDL surveyor, made the first officially recorded ascent of the mountain in 1831.

Two desperate convicts, James Goodwin and Thomas Connolly, were the first white men to get a glimpse of the Lake St Clair region. Escaping in March 1828 from Sarah Island Penal Settlement in Macquarie Harbour on the west coast, they travelled up the Gordon and Franklin rivers in a Huon pine log canoe before heading towards the settled lands to the east. They battled for three weeks through the vast wilderness, passing about 45km south of Cynthia Bay before finally reaching civilisation.

In 1832 William Sharland, another surveyor, became the first white person to see the yet-to-be-named Lake St Clair, an area known to the Aboriginals as *Leeawuleena*, 'Sleeping Water'. It was the Surveyor-General George Frankland, leading an 1835 expedition to seek the source of the Gordon River, who named the lake Lake St Clair, apparently after the St Clair family of Loch Lomond in Scotland. A lover of Greek mythology, Frankland was moved to name the flat-topped mountain beside the lake Mt Olympus, starting a theme heartily taken up by later explorers and bushwalkers.

During the 1860s trappers and prospectors began to stay in the area, building base huts to store their samples and skins. Two of the huts from this era still survive: Old Pelion built in 1917 by the Mount Pelion Mines No Liability Company and Du Cane Hut built by Patrick 'Paddy' Hartnett in 1910.

Hartnett on top of Mt Ossa, 1921 (Tasmanian Archive and Heritage Office)

Hartnett, who had a circuit of huts in the area, including the original Kia Ora Hut, hunted wallabies and possums in the winter when their coats were at their best, drying and selling the skins which ended up in Europe. In late spring he'd burn off his hunting runs in the Mersey and Forth valleys, much as the Aboriginal people always had, then spend summer prospecting and guiding hikers. Hartnett was a popular guide, becoming famous not only for his bush skills, but also for the combination of his red hair, blue eyes and an always-present black bowler hat (which doubled as a drinking vessel). Early prospectors like Hartnett found small amounts of copper, wolfram (tungsten) and coal, but never enough to sustain mining for long.

In 1912 an Austrian, Gustav Weindorfer, and his Tasmanian wife, Kate, started building an alpine chalet called Waldheim, 'forest home', at the edge of a King Billy pine and myrtle forest about 3km from Dove Lake. Keen naturalists, they wanted to share their passion for the area with visitors – a way of promoting their vision for the area to become a national park.

News of the curious chalet tucked deep in the forest soon began attracting intrepid nature lovers who also succumbed to the raw beauty of the area (and its charismatic front man, Weindorfer). By the early 1920s Weindorfer took the national park concept on the road, and assisted by mountaineer and photographer Fred Smithies, gave public lectures across Tasmania displaying Smithies' pictures. As a result of their lobbying 64,000 hectares of land from Cradle Mountain to Lake St Clair were declared a 'scenic reserve and wildlife sanctuary' in 1922.

After the scenic reserve was declared some hunters and snarers began to work as guides, although others continued to snare illegally up until fur prices collapsed in the early 1950s. In 1930 the Cradle Mountain Reserve Board employed the former local fur trapper Bert Nichols to blaze a track from Cradle Mountain to Cynthia Bay. The track incorporated sections of previous routes, including a path from Waldheim to Barn Bluff, mining tracks and Nichols' own snaring routes between the Pelion Plains and Lake St Clair. Of Aboriginal heritage, Nichols was snub-nosed, stockily built and swore like a pirate from beneath his squashed felt hat. He seemed immune to the weather, never bothering with a raincoat even in the worst storms. After blazing the track, Bert wrote to the director of the Tasmanian Government Tourist Bureau, Evelyn Temple Emmett, inviting him to try it out. Emmett, who had been instrumental in having the reserve created, was only too keen, and along with seven friends from the Hobart Bushwalking Club completed the track in January 1931 – the first Overlanders.

Initially Nichols guided all groups on the five-day hike to Lake St Clair, but by 1937 – mostly due to his hard work upgrading the path, huts and bridges – hikers could venture the route alone.

Horses in the snow outside Waldheim, 1929 (Tasmanian Archive and Heritage Office)

Another pioneer of the track was Albert 'Fergy' Fergusson, who ran a tourist camp at Cynthia Bay from the early 1930s until 1946, and operated a speedboat service on Lake St Clair with *Miss Velocity*. His tourist camp featured a dining room where Devonshire teas could be enjoyed surrounded by ferns and mosses.

Fergy, described as having "boundless cheer, innocent watery-blue eyes and a seamed face", was also reputed to have a skull reinforced with tin plate courtesy of an injury sustained while serving in the Light Horse in World War I. He became the first ranger in the Lake St Clair area, earning the accolade of the 'bushman's friend' for his good nature, fine bush skills and reservoir of tall tales. He built the original Pine Valley Hut in 1941–1942 and was apparently so proud of his construction that when a hiker complained of the lack of washing facilities he promptly set off to Hobart to buy a bathtub. After transporting the cast-iron bath to Cynthia Bay he put it in a boat and rowed it across the lake then carried it over 10km to the hut balanced upside down on his shoulders and head. The tub was extremely heavy and, being a warm day, Fergy gradually removed clothing until he was battling along the track in nothing but his boots – which was when he encountered a party of ladies from the Hobart Bird Watching Association.

Fergy's contribution to the development of the Overland is recognised in the naming of Fergys Paddock and Fergusson Falls. His ashes were scattered at the falls in 1970.

When Weindorfer died in 1932 the Connell family, local trappers and friends of the Austrian, took over Waldheim, improving the track, building huts and bridges and continuing Weindorfer's tradition of guiding hikers. In 1935 Lionel Connell became the first permanent ranger appointed by the Cradle Mountain Reserve Board. Lionel, assisted by his four sons, upgraded the northern end of the track, established many of the sidetrips in the area, and built the original Windermere, New Pelion and Kitchen huts. In 1947 the Connells sold Waldheim and its surrounding land for inclusion into the reserve. In the same year the separate boards that administered the north and south of the park were joined to create the Cradle Mountain–Lake St Clair National Park Board.

World Heritage

In 1982 a large part of western Tasmania's wilderness was granted world heritage listing, an area further increased in 1989 and 2013. The Tasmanian World Heritage Area now comprises 1.58 million hectares, including Cradle Mountain–Lake St Clair National Park. It's one of only 25 world heritage sites listed for both natural and cultural values, and one of only two sites that meets seven of the possible 10 world heritage criteria, including Aboriginal archaeological

The dining room at Fergusson's camp, 1936 (Tasmanian Archive and Heritage Office)

and cultural sites revealing the traditions of the world's most southerly population during the last ice age (15,000–20,000 years ago); a valuable record of the earth's evolutionary history; living evidence of the southern supercontinent of Gondwana and its subsequent fragmentation, such as beech trees; on-going natural processes in undisturbed environments; exceptional natural beauty; and providing habitat for rare and endangered flora and fauna, many which are endemic to Tasmania.

GEOLOGY

Getting your head around a few of the geological processes that created Tasmania helps explain the track's landscape, plants and animals. The complete geological story is mind-bendingly complex; this is just a simplified overview.

Gondwana

Around 250 million years ago the supercontinent known as Pangea began to break into a southern landmass called Gondwana, and a northern one called Laurasia. Gondwana comprised the future Australia, New Zealand, South America, India, Madagascar and Africa, while Laurasia contained North America, Europe and Asia. The climate was wet and warm, and relatively simple plants such as conifers and ferns flourished. Amazingly, a few Tasmanian species can trace their lineage all the way back to Pangea, including cave spiders, freshwater crayfish, mountain shrimp, and – arguably – pencil and King Billy pines.

Around 180 million years ago, Gondwana itself began to break up causing huge ructions in the earth's crust. As the lands separated, 1200°C molten dolerite pushed towards the surface, spreading in sheets several hundred metres thick between layers of sedimentary rock. Over millions of years this dolerite shrank and cracked as it cooled, assuming its characteristic columnar appearance, and, over millions of years, the softer sedimentary rock above weathered away to reveal the hard, grey dolerite rock beneath. It's this dolerite that forms the spectacular fluted mountains along the track, such as Cradle Mountain and Mt Ossa. Similar rock is found in South Africa, South America and Antarctica – lingering evidence of the break-up of Gondwana.

Over 100 million years ago, while Gondwana was still in the slow process of breaking up, flowering plants evolved and slowly spread throughout the supercontinent, competing with the conifers. Among the most successful of these Gondwanan flowering plants were the southern beeches, two of which still survive at Cradle Mountain – myrtle and the deciduous beech. Numerous beech species can still be found scattered throughout Australia, Chile, New Caledonia, New Guinea and New Zealand.

Fossils provide further evidence of a common Gondwanan past, such as the fossilised foliage of a giant conifer, *Fitzroya tasmanensis*, found near Cradle Mountain – an extinct relative of a species that only exists today in Chile and Argentina. Animal fossils are rarer, but platypuses and echidnas are both suspected of having Gondwanan ancestors, as fossils of one of their extinct relatives has been found in South America.

India was the first landmass to break away from Gondwana, followed by Africa and New Zealand, and by 65 million years ago only South America, Australia and Antarctica were still joined. Some 45 million years ago Australia finally broke away from Antarctica, its last link with Gondwana, and a major period of faulting formed Bass Strait and many of the valleys, mountains and cliffs we see in Tasmania today.

For 30 million years Australia evolved in isolation, slowly drifting north. The Antarctic Circumpolar Current became established in the new Southern Ocean, freezing Antarctica and making Australia cooler and drier. The temperate rainforests covering most of Australia

Deciduous beech shows autumn colours in late April

slowly retreated to the wetter, mountainous south-east, replaced by drought and fire-adapted eucalypts, banksias, sheoaks and wattles.

Around 15 million years ago Australia began colliding with South East Asia, allowing for an exchange of plants and animals, such as bats and rodents.

Today, Tasmania's relatively mild and wet conditions have made it one of the last refuges for many of Gondwana's ancient plants and animals.

The mark of the glacier

The national park we see today was largely shaped over the last two million years as at least six ice ages came and retreated, each covering much of the landscape under hundreds of metres of ice. The last ice age ended only about 13,000 years ago when temperatures rose and glaciers all over the world retreated, releasing water that raised the sea level by 130 metres and severed Tasmania's land bridge to the mainland.

The Overland is the best place in Australia to see the effects of an ice age. Many of the hills, mountains, valleys and lakes were shaped by ice, a process that also helps explain the distribution of plants and animals.

During the last ice age a 300km^2 icecap covered much of the park. Areas lying beneath this huge weight of ice, like the Cradle Plateau, were worn smooth, while areas above the ice retained their rugged shape, like the peaks of Cradle Mountain, Barn Bluff and The Acropolis.

Smaller 'cirque' glaciers formed on the cooler sides of mountains where snow built up and compacted into ice. These glaciers wore away at the edges of the mountains, creating deep bowl-shaped depressions called 'cirques'. The Overland follows the edge of one such cirque, Cradle Cirque, and passes other examples now filled with water: Crater Lake, Dove Lake and Lake Wilks. A three-kilometre wide cirque can be seen near Bert Nichols Hut, bound by the Du Cane and Travellers ranges.

Eventually these glaciers began to move slowly downhill along river valleys, the enormous weight of the ice loosening rock which was carried along inside the glacier. As the rocks and ice slid over the bedrock it scoured everything beneath like a giant sheet of sandpaper, creating smooth U-shaped valleys such as the Cradle, Pine, Narcissus and Forth valleys, which are noticeably rounded compared with river-worn valleys such as the Mersey.

Lake St Clair was formed when three glaciers – in the Narcissus Valley, Pine Valley and Marion Creek Valley – met with the ice cap to gouge out a deep groove.

When the glaciers began to recede about 10,000 years ago, the boulders that had been carried along by the ice were deposited, often on top of completely different rock far from their original source. These are called 'glacial erratics', and many of the conspicuous boulders along the track are examples of these stranded rocks.

Rock and debris were also deposited at the edges of the melting glaciers, particularly their tips, leaving behind mounds and ridges called 'moraines'.

Cradle Mountain from Cradle Plateau (Stage 1, photo: François Maréchal)

These can be seen near Lake St Clair, both in the Narcissus Valley and near Cynthia Bay, where the track follows their raised, stony ridges (now mostly covered with eucalypts).

Finally, many of the small lakes along the Overland were formed as glaciers retreated and left behind chunks of ice surrounded by moraine material. As this ice melted the depressions in which they lay filled with water to form lakes.

WEINDORFER, WALDHEIM AND THE MAKING OF A NATIONAL PARK

If there is one person today's visitors can thank for preserving the Cradle Mountain area it is Gustav Weindorfer.

Gustav Weindorfer was born in Austria in 1874. An interest in the natural world led him to study farm management, but much to his frustration the only work he could find was as an accountant for a wine merchant. At 25, fed up with the job and craving adventure, he booked a ticket to the distant, unknown land of Australia.

On first sight he wasn't impressed. "The country looks dreadful", he wrote home. "The gum trees, at all times wretched creatures, stood sadly in the drought-stricken country, rattling their long leaves."

He settled in Melbourne where he soon started exploring the countryside with the Victorian Field Naturalists' Club. Another member of the club with similar botanical interests was Kate Cowle, a Tasmanian-born woman 11 years Weindorfer's senior.

Gustav Weindorfer, 1920 (Tasmanian Archive and Heritage Office)

Kate must have liked what she saw: a tall, strong, engaging man with a thick accent and an even thicker handlebar moustache, because in February 1906 they got married. For the wedding they travelled back to Tasmania where Kate had relatives in the north of the state. Within hours of arrival Gustav was fighting bushfires with his future relatives, battling all night to save the homestead in which they were married the next day. Their honeymoon was five weeks in a leaky tent on Mt Roland collecting plant specimens and subsisting on kangaroo tail soup.

Gustav was impressed by Tasmania's rugged scenery, which reminded him of his mountainous homeland. For the first time, far in the distance, he saw the distinctive ridge of Cradle Mountain – and his curiosity was piqued.

But first they settled down, buying some land and starting a farm, growing oats, potatoes, vegetables and fruit, and raising sheep and cattle. Gustav impressed the locals with his good manners, hard work and outgoing personality.

His first trip to Cradle Valley was in January 1909, when Gustav and a Melbourne friend, Charlie Sutton, followed their compass across trackless moorland until they entered Cradle Valley, at that time known to only a few hunters, trappers and some adventurous mountaineers.

Gustav was smitten with the wildness of the highlands and the richness of its flora, with many of the plants yet to be classified. On returning to the farm he wrote an article for the Victorian Field Naturalists describing Cradle Mountain as "a veritable El Dorado for the botanist". Impatient to return, Gustav organised a trip back to the area with Kate and his neighbour Ronnie Smith that December. On 4 January 1910 they climbed Cradle Mountain, Kate, in her long skirt and bone-necked blouse, keeping pace with the men, the first woman known to have reached the summit.

In an article 25 years later, Smith described how Gustav stretched out his arms and declared, "This must be a national park for the people for all time. It is magnificent, and people must know about it and enjoy it."

Excited by Gustav's vision, the party promptly started scouting around for a location to build the chalet, settling on a site at the edge of an ancient myrtle and King Billy pine forest about 3km from Dove Lake.

In March 1912 Gustav started building Waldheim ('forest home' in his native tongue). Waldheim was basic but beautiful: bunks of rough wood and hessian, mattresses stuffed with sphagnum moss, blocks of wood for chairs and a huge fireplace with toasting forks made from twisted fencing wire. His motto hung on the wall, "This is Waldheim, where there is no time and nothing matters".

Visitors soon started arriving, particularly friends from the Victorian Field Naturalists' Club, who endured the rough journey to enjoy Waldheim's rustic charm and the area's mountains, lakes and rainforest. Gustav was cook as well as guide and host, treating guests to his home-baked bread, freshly ground coffee (a rarity in those times) and his specialty – wombat and garlic stew.

Just when custom was beginning to increase, World War I broke out. Fear of foreigners became rife: rumours circulated that the Austrian deep in the highlands was a spy and Waldheim was equipped with a radio transmitter to communicate with the enemy. Kate's health began to deteriorate, doctors advising her of a weak heart. Soon Kate was in and out of hospital, Gustav leaving Waldheim to be by her side. When she died on 29 April 1916, aged 52, Gustav wrote in his diary, "I have lost my best friend". He retreated to Waldheim, drawing solace from hard work and the area's beauty.

By winter 1919 Gustav had completed most of Waldheim's buildings. Visitors in October 1920 included Tasmanian photographer and mountaineer Frederick Smithies and his next-door neighbour Herbert King, another photographer. It's to these two men we owe thanks for much of the photographic record of the area. Smithies, in particular, came to share Gustav's vision of a national park and joined him on a promotional tour of Tasmania showing lantern slides and drumming up support for the idea, including with the Minister of Lands. On 16 May 1922, 64,000 hectares from Cradle Mountain to Lake St Clair were declared a 'scenic reserve and wildlife sanctuary'.

By this time Gustav's heart was giving him trouble, but he continued to host visitors and guide them through the area, in the evenings regaling them with fireside tales about the grand balls and buildings of Vienna. Rather than slowing down because of his bad heart, Gustav speeded up, literally, buying an Indian motorcycle in 1931, which was well suited to the poor tracks leading to Waldheim.

On 5 May 1932 Gustav was found dead. His heart had failed as he had tried to kick-start his motorcycle; he was 58. His friends gathered to bury him in front of the chalet, his grave marked with a simple King Billy pine cross bearing his nickname 'Dorfer'.

In 1976 the National Parks and Wildlife Service, concerned that the buildings were becoming run-down, demolished Waldheim. They were unprepared for the outraged response of hikers from around Australia who regarded the chalet as a special part of Tasmanian bushwalking history. The Parks hired a local builder, Ted Forster, to make a replica, incorporating as much of the original building as could be salvaged. It was fitting that Forster had been taught to split King Billy shingles by Dorfer himself.

PLANTS AND ANIMALS

A separate 'Plant and animal guide' can be found after the route description in this book. It contains detailed information on the Overland's plants, animals, snakes and birds.

Plants

Learning about some of the plants along the track really adds to the Overland experience. The species are not only intrinsically beautiful but also provide an insight into the area's geological, climatic and human history.

Many Tasmanian plants can be traced back to the break-up of Gondwana over 34 million years ago. Today their closest relatives are not always on Australia's mainland, but on some of the other landmasses that once comprised Gondwana, such as New Zealand, South America and New Caledonia.

Separated from the mainland for over 10,000 years, Tasmania has developed many plant species found nowhere else on earth, with over 400 endemic plant species, a third of which can be found in the Cradle Mountain area.

Animals

Tasmania is a refuge for many native animals that are now extinct or threatened on the Australian mainland. The variety and quality of the vegetation along the Overland, combined with the animals' familiarity with hikers, presents a rare opportunity to get close to these creatures.

Summer wildflowers are a highlight for many walkers

Most of the larger animals are marsupials – mammals whose females have pouches for raising their young. Most are also nocturnal. Marsupials such as pademelons and Bennett's wallabies prefer open areas for feeding and can commonly be seen near huts and camping areas in the morning or evening.

DEVILS IN DANGER

In 1995 the population of Tasmanian devils was estimated to be between 130,000 and 150,000. By May 2008 the devil was listed as endangered, with predictions they could be extinct in the wild. This Tasmanian icon – the emblem of the Tasmania Parks and Wildlife Service – is succumbing to a terrible disease: Devil Facial Tumour Disease (DFTD).

DFTD starts as small lesions, or bumps, in and around the mouth of the animal. These develop into large tumours on the face and neck; once the cancer is visible the devil usually dies within months. The disease is transmitted through bites and nips, part of the way devils communicate, and the cancer is unusual in that it's only one of three that spreads like a contagious disease. The problem seems to be that the devil's lack of genetic variety means the animal's immune system doesn't recognise the problem and the cancer grows unchecked.

DFTD covers more than 65 per cent of Tasmania and continues to spread. It is estimated over 80 per cent of the total wild Tasmanian devil population has been lost. In the north-east, where the disease was first discovered in 1996, only around 5 per cent of the population have survived.

To insure the species against extinction, disease-free devils were relocated to large quarantine facilities, including on Maria Island. The success of this program means that the progeny of these devils – vaccinated against the disease – are now being released back into the wild. But these releases have met a mixed fate: some devils have re-established and bred, but others have been killed by traffic or been infected with DFTD – despite the added protection of the vaccine.

Recent surveys show, despite early predictions that the entire wild devil population would become extinct, some devils continue to survive in DFTD areas. Scientists now believe the animals will be able to coexist with the disease, albeit at reduced densities.

To learn more about the efforts being made to help save the Tasmanian devil visit www.tassiedevil.com.au.

Birds

Tasmania has about 220 species of land birds, around 30 of which may be commonly found along the Overland. The diverse woodlands of the Narcissus Valley are a particularly good place to see and hear birds. Of the 12 species found only in Tasmania, 11, such as the black currawong and yellow wattlebird, may be seen along the track.

LOOKING FOR THE LOST

The Tasmanian tiger (or thylacine from its scientific name *Thylacinus cynocephalus*, dog-headed pouched one) had a long, stiff tail like a kangaroo and a yellow-brown coat with black stripes running across its back and rump. Although it resembled a large dog, and had a remarkably similar skull to a red fox, the thylacine was a marsupial – the largest carnivorous marsupial of modern times.

A photo of a thylacine taken in the 1930s (National Archives of Australia)

An adult thylacine weighed between 20 and 30kg and was about 180cm from tip to tail. Despite its fierce nickname, the thylacine was a quiet, placid animal that avoided contact with humans. It had such a nervous disposition that many animals apparently died of shock upon capture. It would growl and hiss when agitated and give a distinctive double 'yap' when hunting wallabies and other animals on the open heaths at night. During the day it retreated to forested areas and sheltered in caves or hollow logs.

Indigenous rock art shows the thylacine was found throughout mainland Australia as well as New Guinea. It appears to have become extinct on the mainland and New Guinea around 2000 years ago due to competition with the introduced dingo and hunting by Indigenous people. Tasmania was the tigers' last refuge.

After white settlers came to the island in 1803 and began introducing stock into prime tiger habitat, thylacines were soon blamed for killing sheep. The first bounty on the thylacine was introduced by the Van Diemen's Land Company in 1830, an idea taken up by the Tasmanian government in 1888 when they introduced a £1 bounty per animal, a sum claimed 2184 times before the bounty lapsed in 1909. Habitat clearing, poisoning, reduced prey, competition from wild dogs and a distemper-like disease are all likely to have contributed to the species' decline. On 7 September 1936, the last known thylacine died in Hobart Zoo. Fifty years later they were officially declared extinct.

Yet there have been numerous thylacine sightings reported since their 'extinction', many of them, surprisingly, from the mainland, and yet others from New Guinea. In Tasmania there have been over 300 reported sightings since 1936. In 1982 a researcher with the Tasmania Parks and Wildlife Service, Hans Naarding, saw what he thought to be a thylacine for several minutes near Arthur River in north-west Tasmania. In 2016 thylacine seekers recorded blurry footage of a stocky animal with a long tail weaving through forest in central Tasmania.

Despite the lack of proof and against all probability, many people continue to nurture a hope that tigers continue to roam somewhere in Tasmania's vast wilderness.

PLANNING YOUR TRIP

WHEN TO GO

Tasmania has four distinct seasons, although on the Overland the characteristic rapid changes in weather mean you might feel like you've experienced them all in the same day. It's a rare Overland trip that doesn't include rain, hail, strong winds or snow, particularly near Cradle Valley where, on average, it rains about five days in seven and snows 54 days a year – including occasionally in summer!

Tasmania is in the path of the 'Roaring Forties', winds that rush around the earth between 40 and 50 degrees latitude. These moisture-laden westerly winds dump copious amounts of rain on the slopes of western Tasmania, leaving the rest of the state relatively dry. The Roaring Forties are also responsible for Tasmania's mild winters and cool summers. The northern part of the Overland can get the worst of the weather as it's higher and more exposed than the south. Check the Bureau of Meteorology's forecast before you set off, www.bom.gov.au. The following weather information is from Cradle Valley and gives an indication of what to expect.

Summer: December, January, February

Summer is arguably the best time to hike the Overland. Many plants are flowering, the days are long – making sidetrips more feasible – and the average maximum temperature is a warm 16.3°C (with a possibility of temperatures in the 30s). The average minimum temperature is 5.1°C.

Summer also has the least rain, 154mm per month on average, about half as much as winter. The conditions are particularly stable from mid January to February. While summer is the busiest time of the year, the booking system ensures that the track is never overrun. If you're planning a summer hike book as early as possible as popular dates fill quickly. Bookings open 1 July each year. See Booking your hike section for more details.

Autumn: March, April, May

In autumn hikers can enjoy the spectacular golds and reds of Australia's only autumn deciduous tree, the deciduous beech (see the Plant and animal guide), with the colours often at their best around Anzac Day (25 April). The track is often less crowded than in summer and the weather is relatively stable, particularly in March. The average maximum temperature is 11°C, the minimum 3.1°C. There is an average of 212mm of rain per month, with the first significant snows usually falling in May. Another bonus of autumn hiking is the wonderful array of fungi on display.

Heavy snow on the plateau near The Acropolis (Stage 6 sidetrip)

Winter: June, July, August

For experienced hikers only. Although Tasmania doesn't have permanent snow cover, it snows frequently enough in winter that the track can be difficult to discern, especially in white-out conditions. It gets dark at 5pm. Overnight temperatures can be as low as -9°C, with an average maximum of 4.9°C, and minimum of -0.3°C. Winter also has the most rain, the monthly average of 299mm making the tracks even wetter and muddier than usual. However, there can still be lovely weather, especially in July, when crisp, clear days reveal spectacular snowy landscapes and each step along the track is into fresh snow (which is when carrying snowshoes can be an advantage).

Spring: September, October, November

September and October are usually the windiest months of the year, with the conditions becoming more stable in November. Some plants begin to flower in late spring, including the 'Christmas decoration' of the bush, the Tasmanian waratah. The average maximum temperature is 10.3°C, the minimum 1.4°C and there's a monthly average of 248mm of rain.

WAYS TO HIKE THE TRACK

There are three ways of hiking the trail: as an independent hiker camping or using the public huts, as part of a registered 'group', or as part of a Cradle Mountain Huts tour group.

For safety reasons it's not recommended to hike the Overland alone, especially the sidetrips, which are less frequented and more dangerous than the main track.

Please note, all prices in this book are in Australian dollars. (One dollar equals roughly 50p.)

Independent hikers

Most hikers complete the track independently, not as part of a commercial tour group. For those familiar with multi-day hikes this is the favoured option as it allows a flexible schedule and is low cost.

Groups

Clubs, community groups, tours, schools and other 'official' groups need to register with Parks Tasmania to use the designated group campsites near each hut. Official groups can book up to two years in advance: contact the Overland Track Administrator (Monday–Friday) for details on 03 6165 4254 or overlandtrack@parks.tas.gov.au.

For non-official groups a maximum group size of eight is recommended as a courtesy to other hikers. All groups are encouraged to camp instead of sleeping in huts. See 'Group camping' for more information.

Commercial tour companies

Joining a tour can have advantages, especially for people who would otherwise be hiking alone. Guides are knowledgeable and helpful, food is provided (making packs lighter), and companies have all the equipment and expertise to ensure a safe, comfortable trip.

Camping tour companies

These tour operators use the designated group camping areas near the huts. In 2019 most charged around $2000–$2400 and took six days to do the walk. Companies include:

- Long-established Tasmanian Expeditions offer self-guided tours in addition to guided tours, www.tasmanianexpeditions.com.au
- Tasmanian Hikes have regular departures over summer, www.tasmanianhikes.com.au
- Tasmanian Photography Workshops combine a trip along the Overland with tuition in landscape photography, www.camblakephotography.com.au
- Tasmanian Wilderness Experiences take seven days to do the Overland, www.twe.travel
- Trek Tasmania leads a range of hikes across Australia, including the Overland, www.trektasmania.com.au
- Wilderness Expeditions Tasmania have a range of Overland experiences, including snowshoeing during winter, www.wildernessexpeditions.net.au.

Cradle Mountain Huts Walk

The Tasmanian Walking Company's Cradle Mountain Huts Walk is different from the other tour groups because they have their own network of huts nestled away off the track. The huts are rustic, but offer luxuries such as hot showers and twin-share rooms. See www.taswalkingco.com.au.

HIKING DIRECTION

From 1 October to 31 May Tasmania Parks and Wildlife Service requires hikers to walk from north to south. This is to help prevent overcrowding and preserve the wilderness experience. The rest of the year hikers can walk either direction. Walking from Cradle Valley means you get the most difficult part of the walk completed first, which means if a day or two is lost to bad weather it can be made up later on. Walking north to south, the toughest climb is on

Stage 1 features a steep climb to Marions Peak

Stage 1 as you pass Marions Lookout to reach the Cradle Plateau, rising from 870m to 1271m over 5km. On subsequent days there are moderate climbs to passes at Pelion Gap and Du Cane Gap. Once you are over Du Cane Gap it's all downhill, with the track becoming flatter as it approaches Lake St Clair.

Another advantage of hiking north to south is that your legs will be track-hardened by the time you're faced with the 17.2km section from Narcissus Hut to Cynthia Bay (if you opt to walk instead of catching the ferry). As most hikers walk from north to south this book is written from that perspective.

If you do elect to walk from south to north, an option only available at the non-peak period from 1 June to September 30, the suggested stages and times in this book are still relevant. Walking south to north has advantages and disadvantages compared to walking the more common north to south direction. Advantages include walking the steepest section of the track at Marions Lookout on the last day instead of the first, thus avoiding the need to haul a full pack up a steep incline. In good weather hiking south to north also provides a more prolonged view of peaks such as Cradle Mountain. Disadvantages include walking against the flow of the majority of hikers and leaving the most exposed section of the hike – Cradle Plateau and Cradle Cirque – until the last day. Leaving this exposed section to the last day limits your ability to take a rest day in the event of bad weather.

DOING THE HIKE WITH KIDS

Many children successfully complete the Overland each year with adult guidance. The youngest child to have completed the Overland was three — and yes, this kid walked the entire way. In general the track is considered suitable for children aged 10 and up — as long as they're well equipped, experienced multi-day hikers. Many of the climbing sidetrips are not suitable for children as they require clambering over large boulders in the vicinity of steep drops. Taking a child who's not properly prepared on a week-long hike is a recipe for tears all round, but for kids who are ready for it, the Overland can be the biggest adventure of their young lives.

PERMITS

In the peak hiking season, from 1 October to 31 May, hikers are required to:

- Book their departure date in advance
- Buy an Overland Track Pass
- Buy a National Parks Pass
- Walk from north to south.

Off-peak, from 1 June to 30 September, hikers can:

- Walk in either direction
- Don't need to book
- Only require a National Parks Pass.

The booking system and the Overland Track Pass were introduced to prevent overcrowding on the track and to help preserve it for future hikers. During peak season up to 60 walkers a day can depart from Cradle Valley: 34 independent hikers (maximum group size of eight), 13 'group' members (using the special group campsites at each hut) and 13 private hut hikers (staying in a private network of huts run by Cradle Mountain Huts).

BOOKING YOUR HIKE

As mentioned, during the peak hiking season (1 October to 31 May) hikers are required to book their departure date and purchase Overland Track and National Park passes. The easiest way to book and pay for your passes is through Tasmania Parks and Wildlife Service's website, www.overlandtrack.com.au. Passes can also be arranged through the Overland Track Administrator on 03 6165 4254.

It is crucial to reserve your desired departure date as early as possible, especially for the popular months of December, January and February, as well as the Easter holidays. With the number of hikers on the track limited to 60 per day, popular departure dates fill up within days of the online booking system opening at 9am 1 July each year. Hikers book their departure date from Cradle Valley, but once on the track they are free to take as many days as they like. If you're just walking part of the track as a day hike, such as from Ronny Creek to Cradle Mountain and back, you don't need an Overland Track Pass.

TRACK BOOKED OUT? DON'T PANIC

What do you do if the Overland Track departure date you want is booked out? If you can't adjust your schedule to find an available date, you can email the Tasmania Parks and Wildlife Service on overland@parks.tas.gov.au asking to be placed on their waiting list for that departure date. If there is a cancellation they will let you know.

Otherwise there are still lots of good options for exploring Cradle Mountain–Lake St Clair National Park and hiking parts of the Overland Track, with no Overland Track Pass required. Options include:

- Hiking the Overland from Ronny Creek, either as a day trip or staying overnight at Scott-Kilvert Memorial Hut, about 2.1km off the Overland Track beside Lake Rodway. From Scott-Kilvert there are numerous further hiking options, including daytrips to Waterfall Valley, Cradle Mountain or Barn Bluff.
- For those with their own transport, it is possible to access and explore the mid section of the Overland Track. A popular option with Tasmanian walkers is to leave their cars to the east of the national park just off Maggs Road and hike 12km along the Arm River Track to New Pelion Hut. From New Pelion there are several brilliant day hikes, including Mt Ossa, Mt Pelion East and Mt Oakleigh.
- Hiking or taking the ferry from Cynthia Bay to Narcissus Hut. From Narcissus continue to Pine Valley Hut (a sidetrip off the main Overland Track) and spend a couple of days enjoying challenging day hikes such as The Acropolis and The Labyrinth.
- Exploring some of the other wonderful walks Tasmania offers, see Appendix C.

Costs and passes

In 2019 the Overland Track Pass cost $200 for an adult and $160 for under 17s, seniors and those with a pension concession. This might seem expensive, but all fees go to the upkeep of the track. In peak season rangers are vigilant about checking passes and you'll be turned back if you don't have one. If you can't afford a pass, consider walking the track out of peak season when a pass is not required or else just walking a portion of the track (see 'Track booked out? Don't panic').

All hikers need a National Parks Pass regardless of when or where they walk the track. It allows entry into all of Tasmania's national parks including Cradle Mountain–Lake St Clair. A Holiday Pass is the best option for Overlanders. There are two types of Holiday Pass: for individuals without a vehicle a $30 Holiday Pass allows eight weeks' access to Tasmania's national parks; for those with a vehicle, a $60 Holiday Pass may represent better value as it covers up to eight people for eight weeks. Annual and daily passes are also available. Passes can be purchased online from Tasmania Parks and Wildlife Service at https://passes.parks.tas.gov.au, over the phone, from national park visitor centres, Tasmanian travel information centres, the Spirit of Tasmania ferry and Service Tasmania shops. Probably the easiest option is to pay for your pass at the Cradle Mountain or Lake St Clair visitor centre before you set off.

Walker registration booth at Ronny Creek (Stage 1, photo: François Maréchal)

Collecting your Overland Track Pass

Overland Track Passes need to be picked up from the Cradle Mountain Visitor Centre. It's important to put some thought into when you intend to collect your pass. If you plan to collect your pass on the same day as heading off along the track, Tasmania Parks and Wildlife Service staff insist you collect it before 2pm (and before 1pm in April and May). This is because they want to ensure you have the 3½–5½ hours of daylight needed to walk from the start of the hike at Ronny Creek to Waterfall Valley Huts, the destination for the first night.

Staying in Cradle Valley the night before your departure can be a good idea. This allows for some time to prepare, as well as an early start on the track next day. If you elect to stay in Cradle Valley, you can collect your Overland Track Pass from the Cradle Mountain Visitor Centre between 3pm and 4pm the day before your departure. See Accommodation in Cradle Valley.

No matter when you collect your passes, all members of your walking group will need to attend the Tasmania Parks and Wildlife Service's pre-departure briefing. This briefing drives home the demands and safety requirements of the walk. In addition, each group needs to complete and sign a Walker Safety Checklist confirming that they are carrying the gear regarded as essential to complete the hike safely: good quality tent, sleeping bag, waterproof jacket, fleece, hat and gloves, pants/thermals, camp clothes in waterproof bag and boots. Parks staff have the authority to withhold an Overland Track Pass if they deem hikers are insufficiently equipped for the conditions on the track.

See Appendix B for more ideas of what gear and clothing to bring on the walk.

SIGNING IN

It's important to sign in and out of the walker registration booths at Ronny Creek and Cynthia Bay and also to record your details in the logbook of each hut you stay in along the track. These details are important if things go wrong and you're reported overdue. Remember to tell someone where you're going and when you'll contact them to let them know you've finished the walk. In other words, someone must report you missing before the authorities start checking the registration and logbooks to see where you might be.

GETTING THERE

Visas

All overseas visitors need a visa for Australia. While New Zealand passport holders can apply for a visa upon arrival, citizens of other countries need to apply before leaving home. For information about Australian visas visit www.homeaffairs.gov.au.

By plane

Tasmania doesn't have an international airport, so overseas visitors need to catch a domestic flight to and from the mainland. Most flights arrive and leave from Launceston or Hobart. For Overlanders walking north to south it can be more convenient to fly into Launceston (as it's closer to Cradle Valley) and out of Hobart (where the buses from Lake St Clair often travel to). Factoring in at least an extra day in both Launceston and Hobart is recommended, as it gives you time to buy supplies and some flexibility in case your Overland takes longer than expected. It also gives you a chance to look around these beautiful towns.

Competition between airlines means there are often some good deals, especially if you book a few months in advance. The four main airlines are Jetstar Airways, Tigerair, Virgin Australia and Qantas. Jetstar flies between Hobart and Melbourne, Sydney and Brisbane, as well as between Launceston and the same three cities. Tigerair flies between Hobart and Melbourne and the Gold Coast. Virgin flies between Hobart and Melbourne, Sydney, Brisbane and Perth, and between Launceston and Melbourne, Sydney and Brisbane. Qantas flies between Hobart and Melbourne and Sydney, and between Launceston and Melbourne. Qantas also has a subsidiary, QantasLink, that flies between Melbourne and Devonport (while Devonport is about 100km closer to the start of the track at Cradle Valley, flights are often more expensive and not all bus companies stop there on their way to Cradle Valley).

Keep in mind that you're not allowed to take stove fuel or gas on flights. Also quarantine restrictions mean you can't bring fresh fruit and vegetables into Tasmania.

By ferry

The Spirit of Tasmania ferries operate between Melbourne (Station Pier, Port Melbourne), on the mainland, and Devonport, on the north-central coast of Tasmania, 85km north-east of Cradle Valley. The ferry is generally more expensive than flying, but it's the only option if you want to take a car.

For most of the year ferries depart at 7.30pm (in both directions), arriving at 6am. On most spring and summer weekends the single 7.30pm departure is replaced by two sailings, at 9am and 9pm, getting to Devonport at 6.30pm and 6.30am respectively. From mid December for the rest of summer, as well as on some public holidays, the dual 9am and 9pm departures sometimes sail during the week as well.

Ferry prices depend on the time of year, whether it is a night or day sailing, and type of accommodation. Sleeping in a reclining chair is one of the cheapest options, costing around $200 one way for an adult in peak season. Outside of peak season there are often cheaper deals. Taking your car is a relative bargain at an extra $119 one way, depending on the size of the vehicle. See www.spiritoftasmania.com.au for the latest ferry schedule and prices.

Please note, the Tassielink Transit buses that used to stop at the Devonport Information Centre and take visitors to Cradle Valley no longer operate.

By car

Taking a car leaves you with the challenge of getting it from one end of the hike to the other. The best option is to leave your car at Lake St Clair, and make your way by bus to Cradle Valley to start your walk. That way your car will be waiting for you when you finish. Unfortunately getting between the start and finish of the Overland by bus isn't easy. From Lake St Clair you'll need to take a bus to Hobart or Launceston, stay overnight then catch the bus to Cradle Mountain in the morning. There are similar difficulties in going from Cradle Valley to Lake St Clair. For larger groups, organising a charter bus to meet you at the end of the hike and return you to your car might be an option: see 'Charter bus' section.

By bus

Getting a bus is by far the most popular way of accessing the track. But beware: some Overlanders get stranded awaiting buses, particularly out of peak season when transport options are limited. Make sure you check bus timetables carefully and book well in advance. Tassielink Transit buses – once the main way of getting to and from the Overland Track – no longer service the walk.

Bus companies with scheduled services

In peak season there are regular bus connections to the Overland from Launceston and Hobart. Outside this period bus services are less frequent and careful planning is required to make sure you don't get stranded. Check schedules and costs with the transport companies and book in advance.

McDermott's Coaches has a daily Launceston to Cradle Valley bus from 1 September to 30 April departing 7.30am and returning 3pm, $75 one way. For the rest of the year they operate a reduced timetable. They also provide charter buses, www.mcdermotts.com.au.

From 1 October to 31 May Overland Track Transport offers a $75 7am mini-bus from Launceston to Cradle Mountain – all the way to the start of the walk at Ronny Creek. From 1 October to 30 April they operate a daily Lake St Clair to Launceston service departing at 2.30pm, $75. From 1 November to 30 April they also provide a daily 2.30pm Lake St Clair to Hobart service, $85. They also provide charter buses, www.overlandtracktransport.com.au.

Charter buses

These 12- or 14-seat mini-vans will drop you off and/or pick you up from the walk; this can be cost-effective for larger groups as the more people you have, the cheaper it becomes per person. It's often worth ringing to see if you can share a ride with another group.

- Cradle Mountain Coaches, www.cradlemountaincoaches.com.au
- Outdoor Tasmania, www.outdoortasmania.com.au
- Overland Track Transport, www.overlandtracktransport.com.au
- Tasmanian Road Trips, www.tassieroadtrips.com
- Transport Tasmania, part of Tasmanian Wilderness Experiences, www.twe.travel.

ACCOMMODATION AND FACILITIES AT THE START OF THE TRACK

Cradle Valley isn't actually a town, more a loose string of accommodation options in the thick bushland near the park entrance. The area is often referred to as Cradle Mountain, but the mountain itself is about 12km south of the national park boundary.

Cradle shuttle bus service

Visitors with vehicles need to leave them at the Cradle Mountain Visitor Centre and take the shuttle bus into the park. The Cradle Mountain Visitor Centre is located 2km from the park boundary and 7.5km from Dove Lake. (Scheduled bus services terminate at the Visitor Centre, apart from the Overland Track Transport shuttle that pauses at the Visitor Centre before continuing to the start of the Overland at Ronny Creek.)

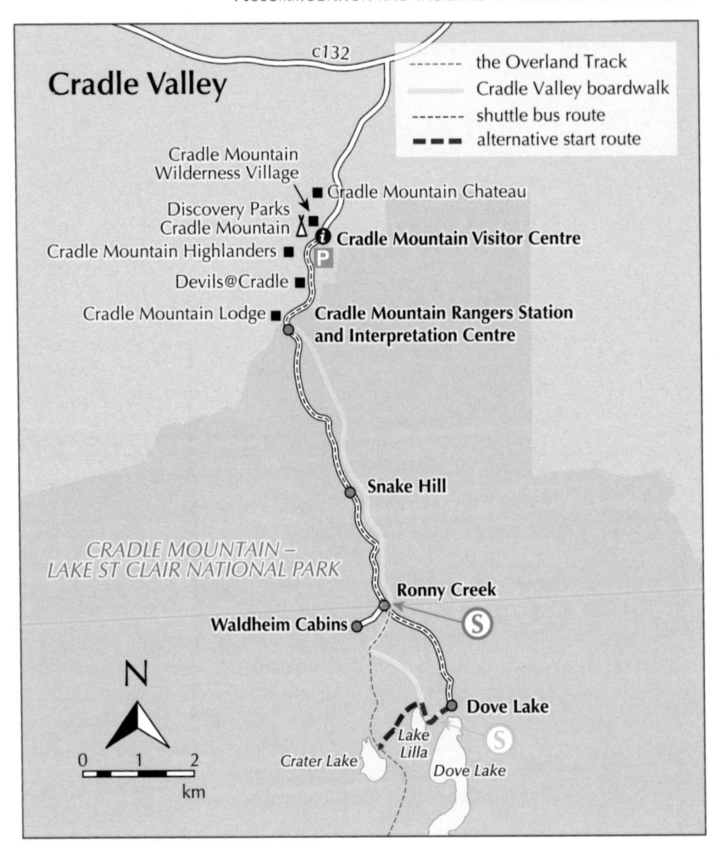

The shuttle bus leaves from beside the Visitor Centre's information office, and makes four stops: Cradle Mountain Ranger Station and Interpretation Centre, Snake Hill, Ronny Creek (for the start of the Overland) and Dove Lake (which has good views of Cradle Mountain and is an alternative start for the Overland). You can use the shuttle bus service for free with your National Parks Pass.

Timetables for the shuttle bus vary from season to season but the service usually operates throughout the year. During December and January the shuttle runs from 8.15am to 6.40pm departing every 5–10 minutes from

The lovely Wombat Pool is on the alternative start from Dove Lake (Stage 1)

both the Visitor Centre and Dove Lake ends. The last bus from Dove Lake is at 7pm. In winter there are buses from 9.30am to 4.30pm departing every 30 minutes. Services can change with demand: check with Cradle Mountain Visitor Centre on 03 6492 1110.

Alternatively there's a beautiful meandering boardwalk leading from Cradle Mountain Rangers Station and Interpretation Centre to Dove Lake via Ronny Creek. It's 5.5km to Ronny Creek and an extra 3km to Dove Lake.

Cradle Mountain Visitor Centre

McDermott's Coaches and charter buses will drop you at the Cradle Mountain Visitor Centre where you'll need to show your receipt to collect your National Parks Pass, or else pay for it there. In peak season you'll also need to show your Overland Track booking receipt to collect your Overland Track Pass. Exactly when you collect your Overland Track Pass needs some careful thought: see 'Collecting your Overland Track Pass'.

Opening hours for the Visitor Centre are from 8am to 5pm in peak season. In winter, the Visitor Centre opens at 9am.

The centre offers 30 minutes free Wi-Fi. See the 'Phones and Wi-Fi' section for more Wi-Fi options.

A fancy new visitors centre – part of a Cradle Mountain Gateway Precinct – is tentatively due to be completed in February 2020. It will have a room dedicated to Overland Track departures.

Cradle Mountain Ranger Station and Interpretation Centre

The Interpretation Centre provides more information on the national park than is available in the Visitor Centre, including on history, and flora and fauna, as well as a topographic model of Cradle Valley and a video about the reserve. The centre, located near the boundary of the national park, is open from 8.30am to 4.30pm in peak season and 9am to 4pm in winter.

Hiking supplies and meals

There's a limited range of hiking supplies available in Cradle Valley and they're very expensive. Try to buy all your supplies in Hobart or Launceston before the walk.

If you do need to top up on food, Discovery Parks Cradle Mountain (opposite the Visitor Centre) has a kiosk open from 8am to 6pm between 1 October and 30 April and 8.30am to 5pm the rest of the year. They sell basic supplies, as does the shop at Cradle Mountain Lodge. The Visitor Centre also stocks a small range of hiking supplies including fuels, sunscreen, jackets, hats and thermals. For a pricy coffee, light meal or snack there's the Cradle Mountain Cafe in the Visitor Centre building. It's open 9am to 5pm (kitchen shutting at 4pm), with reduced hours out of peak season. It also sells petrol.

The tavern at Cradle Mountain Lodge offers lunch and dinner in a hearty atmosphere with open fires. The lodge also has a more expensive restaurant, as does Cradle Mountain Hotel up towards the junction with the highway. Hellyers Restaurant at Cradle Mountain Wilderness Village prepares dinners Tuesday to Saturday, as well as breakfasts every day.

Accommodation in Cradle Valley

If you want an early start, or to spend a few days exploring the many shorter walks around Cradle Mountain, you might consider staying in Cradle Valley. Accommodation options range from bush camping to four-star luxury. Prices are at their highest over summer and other peak times such as Easter (when it's essential to book ahead) while off-season prices can be considerably cheaper, particularly for the more luxurious options.

No camping is allowed inside the national park until you reach Waterfall Valley Huts or Scott-Kilvert Memorial Hut. If you're staying a few days you may want to check out devils@cradle, a facility whose aim is to view, conserve and educate the public about Tasmanian devils. See www.devilsatcradle.com for further information.

The following accommodation options are arranged from cheapest to most expensive. The cheapest option is a campsite at Discovery Parks Cradle Mountain at $53 per night for two people, while at the other end of the scale you can pay nearly $1000 per night for Cradle Mountain Lodge's most luxurious cabin. The average price for a double room or cabin in Cradle Valley is around $200–$300, making Waldheim Cabins' four-, six- or eight-berth rooms great value at $95, $135 and $185 per night respectively.

Discovery Parks Cradle Mountain, across the road from the Visitor Centre and 2km from the park entrance, is the only place in the valley to camp. There's a small shop, camp kitchen, a phone, Wi-Fi and a laundry. For two people it's relatively economical for a campsite nestled in the bush, with clean, modern toilets nearby. The holiday park also has a range of cabins and cottages sleeping four, five or six, as well as backpacker accommodation. See www.discoveryholidayparks.com.au for further information.

Waldheim Cabins, managed by the Tasmania Parks and Wildlife Service, are the only accommodation inside the national park. The cabins are 5.5km from the Cradle Mountain Visitor Centre, about 700m from Ronny Creek car park where the Overland starts. The eight basic cabins are behind a replica of Waldheim Chalet, the former home of Kate and Gustav Weindorfer. The Weindorfers were instrumental in protecting this area and the chalet is now a museum commemorating their life. The four-, six- and eight-berth cabins offer good value for groups. Basic cooking facilities and heating are provided. Bring or hire bedding and linen. Keys can be picked up from the Visitor Centre after 1pm or left for collection in an after-hours key safe at the entrance of the Cradle Mountain Visitor Centre. For more information go to www.cradleinfo.com.au.

Cradle Mountain Highlanders has 16 pleasingly rustic shingle cabins set in beautiful bushland about 300m from the Cradle Mountain Visitor Centre. The self-contained cabins vary in design and level of luxury, reflected in a range of prices. The owners can provide a filling breakfast. For more information see www.cradlehighlander.com.au.

Cradle Mountain Hotel, about a kilometre north of the Visitor Centre, is a large conference centre-like complex on a hillside. It has 60 rooms with woodland views, bar, Wi-Fi, photography gallery and restaurant. It's owned by the Royal Automobile Club of Tasmania (RACT), and offers a 15 per cent discount to interstate and international auto club members. Go to www.cradlemountainhotel.com.au for more information.

Cradle Mountain Wilderness Village, just north of the Visitor Centre, has 37 self-contained cottages in five styles. It also has a restaurant, Hellyers. See www.cradlevillage.com.au for more information.

Cradle Mountain Lodge, part of the Peppers hotel chain, is about 1km south of the Cradle Mountain Visitor Centre near the Ranger Station and Interpretation Centre. The lodge comprises 92 cabins, a restaurant, spa, small store, bar and a bistro/

lodge. The lodge's tavern is a cosy place for a drink or meal. Go to www.cradlemountainlodge.com.au for more information.

ACCOMMODATION AND FACILITIES AT THE END OF THE TRACK

In terms of facilities, there's not much in Cynthia Bay, the small town at the south end of Lake St Clair, apart from the Lake St Clair Visitor Centre (open 8am–5pm in peak season, 9am–4pm the rest of year), the jetty and Lake St Clair Lodge. The Visitor Centre has free Wi-Fi. There are several good short walks in the area.

The small town of Derwent Bridge is 5km from Cynthia Bay. It has a hotel, café, petrol and cabin accommodation.

Lake St Clair ferry

The ferry across Lake St Clair is an option to get to and from Cynthia Bay from Narcissus Hut. Taking the ferry replaces Stage 7 of the Overland Track.

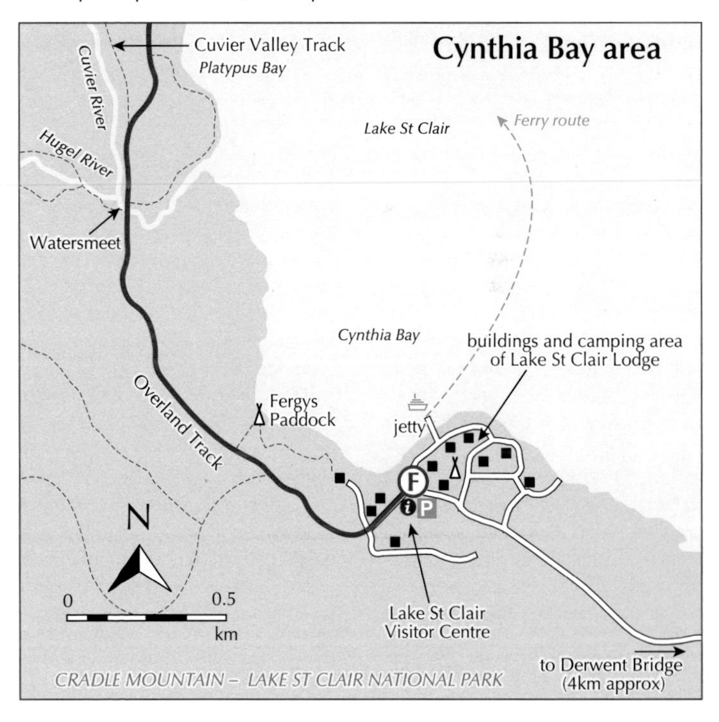

The Ida Clair ferry crosses Lake St Clair between Narcissus Hut and Cynthia Bay (Stage 6)

If you're planning on catching the ferry from Narcissus Hut to Cynthia Bay, book in advance as the boat is often full, especially in summer. Advance bookings can be made on 03 62 891 137 or sceniccruises@lakestclairlodge.com.au.

When you arrive at Narcissus Hut phone or use the hut's radio to confirm your booking (don't worry if you've taken more time on the track and missed your ferry, there's no cancellation fee, but you'll need use the radio to book another spot).

The 20–30 minute ferry trip costs an extortionate $50 for adults and $25 for children (or $42 to be dropped at Echo Point Hut from Cynthia Bay). See 'Stage 6 Bert Nichols Hut to Narcissus Hut' for a ferry schedule and additional information.

Hiking supplies and meals

The café and restaurant in the Lake St Clair Visitor Centre are open 7am–9pm in summer and 8am–8pm the rest of the year, with last order for food half an hour before closing time. The café and restaurant also sell souvenirs and a meagre range of overpriced hiking supplies.

The atmospheric **Derwent Bridge Wilderness Hotel** does hearty breakfasts, lunches and dinners, including famous Sri Lankan curries.

The popular **Hungry Wombat Café** in Derwent Bridge is open 8.00am–6pm in summer, 9am–4.30pm in winter. The kitchen shuts around half an hour before closing time. The Wombat does the best burgers around.

Accommodation in and near Cynthia Bay

There's free camping for Overlanders at **Fergys Paddock** beside Lake St Clair, 660m west of the information centre. The only facilities at the campsite are a toilet and a nice lake to swim in (if you can handle the cold).

Lake St Clair Lodge is run from a reception desk within the Visitor Centre restaurant, open 8am–8pm in summer and 8.30am–5.30pm in winter. They offer campsites, dorm beds and cottages. There are dollar-coin hot showers, a camp kitchen and laundry facilities. The brushtail possums here are the size of wombats – if you are camping, secure your food in the camp kitchen.

The lodge's cheapest option is the bush campsites among the trees near the lake. Campsites can fill up in peak season, especially at weekends, so consider booking ahead. You can also get a bed in a four-bed dorm or a double room, both with access to a shared kitchen and bathroom. The lodge also has 42 cabins scattered through the trees, see www.lakestclairlodge.com.au.

Derwent Bridge Wilderness Hotel is in the hamlet of Derwent Bridge, 5km from Cynthia Bay. It's a large wooden homestead with plenty of character and a roaring fire. They have double rooms in the hotel (including a free continental breakfast) or basic – but cheap – 'bushwalker' rooms in a nearby block. There are meals available in the hotel, www.derwentbridgewildernesshotel.com.au.

Derwent Bridge Chalets and Studios, about 700m from the Derwent Bridge Hotel, have three-and-a-half star self-contained cabins and chalets. Their Olympus Chalet has three bedrooms and accommodates up to eight people, www.derwent-bridge.com.

Four kilometres from Cynthia Bay, on the edge of Lake St Clair, is the discreet luxury resort of **Pumphouse Point**, www.pumphousepoint.com.au. The resort has 19 stylish rooms, some within the prominent art deco hydroelectric building at the end of the jetty. They sometimes require a two-night stay. Their prices include breakfast, and they can also provide guests (and guests only) with lunch and dinner. From Cynthia Bay the resort is about an hour's walk around the lakeshore or via the road. They also pick up and drop off guests from the Visitor Centre.

If you are looking for an additional diversion in the area, many people find **The Wall in the Wilderness**, 2km north-east of Derwent Bridge, worth the $15 entry fee. The Wall is a 100m long, 3m high history of Tasmania being carved into Huon pine panels – an immense 10 year, one man effort, www.thewalltasmania.com.au.

ACCOMMODATION AND FACILITIES ON THE TRACK

Huts

The rustic huts along the track are a highlight for many Overlanders who enjoy the opportunity to meet other hikers from around the world. The huts are basic: no electricity, no lighting, no rubbish bins, no cooking equipment, no bedding and no toilet paper. What they do have are sleeping platforms like giant shelves, rainwater tanks, gas or coal heaters, communal benches and tables, and a nearby composting toilet. Each hut also has a logbook for hikers to record their names and itineraries, as well as a hut journal for reflections or drawings inspired by the walk.

Huts are first come, first served, but nobody can be refused a space. Having made a peak-season booking doesn't allocate you a bed in a hut; bookings just control the number of hikers on the track, which means huts are less likely to become overcrowded. Huts still get very busy in peak season, particularly when it rains. At busy times huts' verandas can make a decent place to sleep.

There are also four emergency shelters along the Overland: Kitchen Hut, the Cirque Emergency Shelter (near the junction with the Lake Rodway Track), Old Pelion Hut (actually just off the main track) and Du Cane Hut. They are great places to take a break, but are only to be used overnight in case of emergency. Other huts you might see along the track are for rangers, Cradle Huts' private cabins or accommodation used by track maintenance workers.

The interior of Windermere Hut is typical of those along the track (Stage 2)

If starting the Overland from Cradle Valley many hikers spend their first night in Waterfall Valley Huts, before sleeping in Windermere Hut, New Pelion Hut, Kia Ora Hut, Bert Nichols Hut and finally Narcissus Hut (or else getting the ferry and spending their last night in Cynthia Bay). This sequence doesn't take into account rest days or the recommended overnight sidetrip to Pine Valley Hut (see 'Stage 6 Bert Nichols Hut to Narcissus Hut'). Fit hikers with limited time often skip a hut or two.

Most huts have water tanks. The exceptions are Old Pelion Hut and Echo Point Hut which have water sources nearby, while Kitchen Hut, Du Cane Hut and the Cirque Emergency Shelter do not have water sources. Everyone likes arriving at clean, tidy accommodation so please sweep out the hut and wipe down the benches before you leave.

There's more information about the individual huts in the track notes and in 'The Overland huts' table at the start of the book.

Heating in the huts

With winter temperatures sometimes dropping to -9°C, all huts (apart from emergency huts) have either coal or gas heating. Given that supplies of gas or coal are limited and need to be labouriously brought in by helicopter, it is important to minimise fuel use, with hikers requested to only use heaters if the hut's thermometer is below 10°C.

Coal for the coal heaters is provided in hoppers near each hut. Coal fires need to be started with kindling – remember to collect some for the next

Narcissus Hut (Stage 6)

Camping platform near Kia Ora Hut (Stage 4)

hikers and to empty out the ash before leaving. The Overland's coal heaters are gradually being replaced by gas heaters. Gas heaters work on timers which automatically shut off after 45 minutes. The new hut at Waterfall Valley, due for completion in May 2020, will feature an environmentally friendly ceramic core heat exchanger.

Camping

Carrying a good quality tent is strongly recommended. Tents are usually warmer, quieter and more private than huts, and you can still use the huts to cook and socialise. If you get into trouble on the track the shelter of a tent could save your life.

Raised wooden platforms for erecting tents are provided near most huts. While putting up your tent on a platform can initially seem odd, they keep campers out of the mud and minimise damage to vegetation. Instead of securing your tent with pegs, platforms have adjustable chains to attach to peg loops, which – along with the rings and nails around the edges of the platforms – make putting up most tents easy. The metal plates on the edges of the platforms are for fuel stoves. Don't camp on the large wooden platforms marked with an 'H' – they're helicopter landing pads!

Rangers strongly encourage hikers to camp at the designated areas near each hut, rather than wild camp in the bush. The only campsite not near a hut is a free campsite for Overlanders at Fergys Paddock, 660m from Cynthia Bay at the end of the walk.

Group camping

Clubs, tours, schools and other 'official' groups can register with Parks Tasmania to use the group campsites near each hut (see 'Groups'). The maximum size of an official group is 13. Group campsites have raised wooden platforms, the same as regular campsites, but they're usually larger and more private, allowing the group to camp together. In peak season, if no group has booked to use the platforms, track rangers may allow other hikers to use the space – but ask first.

Non-official groups camp at the regular campsites. A maximum group size of eight is recommended as a courtesy to other hikers. Groups are encouraged to camp instead of sleeping in huts.

Toilets

There are toilets at all overnight sites, most with a rainwater tank for hand washing. Toilet paper is NOT supplied, so bring your own. All toilets use a waterless composting system that requires the removal of solid and liquid waste by helicopter – an expensive option, but one that ensures no contamination of nearby waterways. The waste is stored in sealed fibreglass pods called 'sputniks' and flown out during autumn. After using a composing toilet add a small cupful of rice hulls from the tub provided – this will help waste and food scraps decompose.

If you need to go to the toilet between sites, dig a 15cm deep hole at least 100m away from any lake or creek and then cover your waste with soil. On pee-stops you are requested to take your used toilet paper or sanitary products out with you in a ziplock bag. Don't burn your toilet paper as this has started bushfires in the past.

The composting toilet at Bert Nichols Hut (Stage 5)

PLANNING DAY-BY-DAY

USING THIS GUIDE

To help plan your hike – and as a handy reference during the walk – this guide contains an overview map and two route summary tables (one for the main track, the second for the sidetrips) at the start of the book.

The main section of the book contains detailed track notes for each day, arranged in the most common hut-to-hut sequence, for example Ronny Creek to Waterfall Valley Huts is given as Stage 1, Waterfall Valley Huts to Windermere Hut as Stage 2 and so on. Read the track notes before you embark on each section, so you are aware of the challenges and features of the day's walk.

An information box at the start of each section contains a summary of the day's walk, including distance, ascent and descent, grade, estimated walking time, maximum altitude and potential sidetrips (walks leading off from the main track). Similar information is provided for each sidetrip. Sidetrip text is differentiated from main track text by a pale blue vertical line at the edge of the page.

All times in this book are for the average walker, who needs the odd break to catch their breath and likes to pause occasionally to soak it all in. Times don't include meal breaks such as lunch. Longer days tend to have wider time ranges, such as the 17.2km Stage 7 which is 5-7hr. This time range reflects the difference between a slower walker and a faster walker across a relatively long day. On shorter days this time difference is less pronounced. The exception is Stage 1 which is not a long day in terms of distance, but walkers have a full pack and face a steep, tough climb up to Marions Lookout. All distances were measured – and re-measured – by GPS.

Each day's walk and potential sidetrip has a 'grade' providing a guide to how difficult the walk is. 'Easy' means a relatively level walk or, if steep, the steep parts are fairly short. 'Medium' involves more sustained steep sections, sometimes with sections of boulder scrambling. A 'hard' grade means long, very steep climbs with some difficult scrambling over boulders that will challenge even experienced hikers.

Route maps and profiles are provided for each day's walk. Bold text within the route descriptions indicates route highlights such as points of interest, viewpoints or good rest spots. These features are also shown on the 1:50,000 map that accompanies the start of each day's track notes. Ideally you should supplement the maps in this book by a waterproof 1:100,000 map (see 'Maps' section).

Views are often referred to in the route descriptions, which can

The incredible stone spires of The Acropolis and the conical peak of Mt Geryon (Stage 6 sidetrip)

be exasperating when the track is shrouded in cloud or fog (as it often is) – but if the weather is clear you'll have some guide to the peaks and valleys you're looking at.

The route descriptions also make reference to plants along the track, with many of these plants detailed in the Plant and animal guide. Learning a few of these species will add an extra dimension to your understanding and enjoyment of the track.

The book's other appendices are designed to assist planning your hike. Appendix A list some useful contacts including accommodation and transport providers, while Appendix B gives lists of suggested food and equipment to take on your walk. And if you are wondering what to do when you have completed the Overland Track, Appendix C has some suggestions for other hikes in Tasmania.

Every effort has gone into ensuring all information is accurate, but – like the Tasmanian weather – things change frequently. Please use the websites and phone numbers provided in Appendix A to confirm the latest.

WHAT TO TAKE

Gear

Make sure you have all your food and equipment before you arrive at the start of the walk, as the choice in Cradle Valley and Cynthia Bay is limited and expensive. Consider each piece of equipment carefully – remember you're going to carry it at least 62.5km. A rough rule of thumb is that most people find a load between one-fifth and one-third of their body weight reasonably comfortable, depending on their fitness. Even with good packing the average backpack will weigh between 16 and 22kg at the start of a week's walk.

See Appendix B for a suggested gear list.

Clothes

The Overland's variable weather means you need to carry a broader range of clothing than for most other hikes. Don't skimp on warm clothing – hypothermia claims lives in Tasmania, even in summer. Many hikers use three layers to keep warm: a close-fitting shirt against the skin, an insulating layer over this – such as a woollen jumper or synthetic fleece – and then a waterproof outer 'shell' layer to protect against wind, rain and snow. For the lower-half it's a similar principle. Cotton, down and many synthetic fibres can lose up to 90 per cent of their insulating ability when wet, and when you add windchill this can quickly drain heat from the body. Also, these materials get heavy when wet and are difficult to dry. Materials such as wool – particularly fine merino – or modern 'micropile' fabrics such as polypropylene perform much better, keeping you warm even when damp. Wearing several layers is the key, as it allows you to easily adjust your temperature by adding or removing garments.

See Appendix B for a suggested clothing list.

Through the buttongrass heading towards the River Forth Lookout (Stage 3)

FOOD AND WATER

Food

Planning your meals means you won't have to beg for food beyond Stage 4 or end up carrying kilograms more than you need. Factor in eating about 20 per cent more than usual – you'll have a healthy appetite on the track! Avoid cans and glass: they're heavy and you'll have to carry them out too. Also avoid anything that has to be cooked for too long as it will use up too much fuel.

If flying in to Tasmania, you can minimise excess luggage fees by getting supplies in Launceston or Hobart. This also avoids any quarantine issues: you can't bring fresh fruit or vegetables from the mainland into Tasmania. Repackage food before starting the hike to avoid carrying excess packaging. Measuring individual meal portions into zip-lock bags – for example, portions of oats, rice and pasta – is convenient and avoids the problem of accidently using too much in any one meal. With careful packing, the total weight of food per day per person can be well under a kilo.

Don't bury food scraps; animals dig them up and human food doesn't agree with them. While excess biodegradable food can be put down the composting toilets along the track, rangers would prefer you carry it out.

See Appendix B for some food ideas.

Water

Access to water isn't a problem on the Overland. Huts have rainwater tanks and, providing hikers use them sparingly, there's usually enough to last over summer. Numerous creeks also cross the track, meaning carrying a one litre water container will usually suffice. Both the tank and creek water is likely to be about the best water you'll ever drink.

Given it's sourced from such a remote, pristine area most people don't bother filtering or purifying it, although this means taking a small but real risk – there's always the chance of an impurity, and getting gastro on a lengthy hike like the Overland is a nightmare. The chances of this can be minimised by drinking only tank

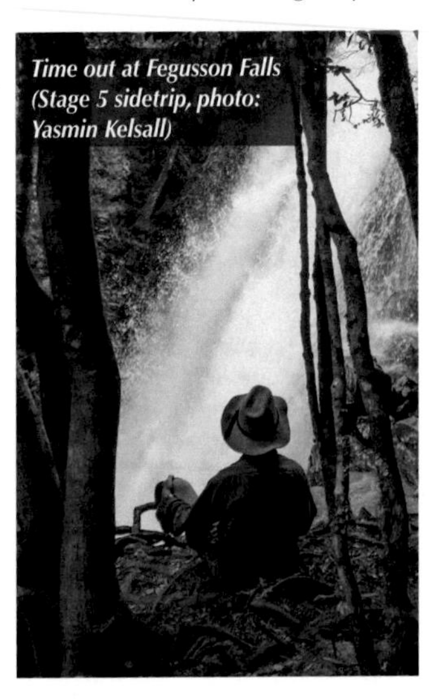

Time out at Fegusson Falls (Stage 5 sidetrip, photo: Yasmin Kelsall)

Natural and manmade track markers (Stage 6 sidetrip)

water, or, if you have to, fill up from a fast-flowing stream above the track. Avoid collecting water from streams at popular rest areas, where people – unfortunately – are more likely to have gone to the toilet. Also avoid swimming where water might be used for drinking further downstream.

Parks Tasmania indemnifies itself by recommending hikers boil all water for three minutes or treat it with a purifier.

Washing

The grease traps beneath the water tanks' taps are designed to treat waste water, so make sure all dish-washing water and toothpaste goes into them. Don't bother with using washing detergent, even biodegradable types affect the environment; hot water and a good scourer will work.

When swimming in streams or rivers, swim downstream from overnight sites and avoid using soap as it harms aquatic life.

WAYMARKING

One of the attractions of the Overland Track is that the main trail is relatively distinct and well maintained. More than 37 per cent of the track – some 30km – is along some form of board-walk, making navigation easy. All track junctions are signposted, providing further clarity for walkers.

While the main trail is relatively well marked, the same can't always be said of sidetrips, where the track can be indistinct and markers few and far between. This is especially true of Mt Oakleigh and the notorious

Labyrinth. For more on sidetrips see the 'Sidetrips' section.

Getting lost – even on the main track – is a real hazard, especially during thick fog or heavy rain. Always carry a map and compass, and consider taking a GPS.

MAPS

In addition to the maps in this guide, it's strongly recommended that you carry a copy of Tasmap's excellent waterproof Cradle Mountain–Lake St Clair 1:100,000 map, available from https://tasmap.tas.gov.au or the Cradle Mountain Visitor Centre.

GPX tracks

GPX tracks for the routes in this guidebook are available to download free at www.cicerone.co.uk/1013/GPX. A GPS device is an excellent aid to navigation, but you should also carry a map and compass and know how to use them. GPX files are provided in good faith, but neither the author nor the publisher accept responsibility for their accuracy.

SIDETRIPS

The sidetrips are optional walks that lead off from the main spine of the Overland. They contain many of the track's most memorable experiences. Sidetrips, particularly the climbs, are much more challenging than the main track and you need to be fit and properly prepared. To help you decide whether to take a sidetrip or not, they have been graded into easy, medium or hard.

The top of The Acropolis with Lake St Clair in the background (Stage 6 sidetrip)

Be aware that sidetrips are less frequented than the main track and are not as well marked. Watch carefully for markers and/or cairns indicating the route, particularly towards the summit of climbs where they're easily overlooked. Climbing sidetrips should only be attempted in reasonably good weather: if it's wet or icy, leave it for another day. A good rule of thumb is if you can't see the top of the mountain don't bother doing the sidetrip – you won't get a view anyway. It's also not advisable to do climbing sidetrips in strong winds as the mountain tops are very exposed.

Leave plenty of time, both to enjoy the sidetrip and to avoid the possibility of getting lost in the dark. Leave your main pack in a hut or near the track junction and take a daypack, or share a backpack among friends, as most of the mountains have sections that require free hands for climbing over boulders. Take plenty of water, sunscreen, a compass/GPS, Personal Locator Beacon (PLB), map, waterproofs, warm clothes, food and a first aid kit.

HEALTH, SAFETY AND EMERGENCIES

Although 9000 people successfully complete the Overland each year, the track's challenge shouldn't be underestimated. Since 2000 at least five people have died on the track,

Bridge over Cephissus Creek (Stage 6 sidetrip)

mostly from falls or hypothermia. If the terrain is getting too difficult, turn back. There are often easier, alternative viewpoints on the sidetrips that still have great views.

In case of emergency, get to a hut or send someone there for help. In peak season there are three track rangers along the Overland at any one time and a WildCare volunteer at Waterfall Valley Huts. All track rangers and WildCare volunteers have either a satellite phone or a VHF radio. Some tour guides, like those from Cradle Huts, also carry satellite phones. The hazards of the walk mean that many hikers elect to carry a PLB (see 'Personal Location Beacons').

Always leave your hiking itinerary with someone – you need to be reported missing before a search begins.

Emergencies

In Australia 000 is the number for emergency services. Triple zero calls automatically access the full range of mobile networks – not just your own – maximising your chance of getting mobile reception. For extra security many hikers carry a Personal Locator Beacon.

PERSONAL LOCATOR BEACONS

Personal Locator Beacons (PLBs) are a type of beacon that, when activated, emit a distress signal that's picked up by satellite and forwarded to local rescue authorities. The authorities, guided by the beacon's continuing signal, will then come looking for you. PLBs should only be used as a last resort in life-threatening situations. They require a relatively open area to ensure a clear signal.

While many types of locator beacons are designed for boats (usually referred to as Emergency Position Indicating Radio Beacons, or EPIRBs), PLBs are designed for hikers and are therefore smaller and lighter. Models with an integral GPS are best, as they give a greater degree of accuracy to guide rescue teams. Australians who purchase a PLB should register it with the Australian Maritime Safety Authority for a faster response in an emergency.

PLBs can be rented from Service Tasmania shops in Hobart, Launceston, Burnie and Devonport. They can also be rented from the Cradle Mountain and Lake St Clair visitor centres, and can be picked up at Cradle Mountain and dropped back at Lake St Clair, or vice versa, costing $40 for 7 days rental. The number of PLBs at the visitor centres is limited, and they can't be reserved. Overland Track Transport also rent PLBs for $50.

Getting lost

The best way of avoiding getting lost is to stay on the main track. Remain with your hiking group, regularly check your map and allow plenty of time to arrive at your hut before dark.

Sidetrip tracks are narrower and sometimes poorly defined; in conditions of limited visibility the path can be difficult to discern. As mentioned, only do the sidetrips, particularly the climbing sidetrips, when there's fair visibility – and remember that conditions can change rapidly. Even with good visibility it's possible to become disoriented, particularly in a confusing landscape like The Labyrinth or poorly marked rainforest. If you do become lost, stop walking. If you're confident you can retrace your steps then do so, otherwise consult your map and compass, looking for features that will tell you your position. If you're still not confident about your location, set up camp. Any pattern of three is a distress call in Tasmania – use it to signal for help with three whistle blasts, three yells or three torch flashes.

Hassles and dangers posed by wildlife

You need to guard your food carefully against nocturnal raiders such as possums, mice and quolls which can chew through backpacks or rip into tents in search of food. Don't keep food or rubbish inside your tent as possums will smell it and keep you awake with repeated attempts to get at it. Storing food and rubbish in the huts is a better idea, but even there possums occasionally break in, forcing out the flywire in a window or sneaking in through a door. Huts – especially older ones – are also sometimes home to native long-tailed mice or other rodents, which are quite adept at climbing into backpacks in search of a feed. Hanging a food bag from the hut's rafters by a piece of string is the best way of keeping your food to yourself.

Nocturnal raiders don't end there. A few possums have even learned to open zips in their search for food and will systematically root through backpacks left in tent vestibules overnight – even if they don't actually contain anything edible. To avoid this, consider hanging your pack in a hut or else securing zips with carabineers or string.

Not all raiders come out at night. Currawongs and ravens can also open zips and delight in opening packs left unattended while hikers are on sidetrips, picking through pockets for anything edible. They can make a real mess. If leaving your bag unattended at a track junction put your pack cover over it for protection. Pack covers that fasten tightly with a drawstring work best as – incredibly – the birds are often deft enough to dislodge loose-fitting covers in their quest for a heist.

March flies

These stocky flies, 15–20mm in length, are at their most common mid January to early March. While

WILDLIFE: IF YOU LOVE IT, LEAVE IT

The feeding of animals has led some creatures – particularly possums, quolls, wallabies, currawongs and ravens – to associate humans with food. This has created a problem for hikers as they now have to defend their food against determined animal raiders. But it's an even bigger problem for the animals, which suffer health problems from this unnatural processed diet, including lumpy jaw, a potentially fatal disease affecting wallabies. Animals that become accustomed to being fed over the busy summer months can face starvation in the off-season when there are fewer hikers, and if they try to return to their former home range it's too late – it's often been occupied in their absence.

their bite is usually only a mild annoyance, some people suffer an allergic reaction to it – another good reason to carry antihistamines. The best protection is to cover your arms and legs with loose-fitting clothes and use insect repellent.

Leeches

Leeches are black worm-like creatures, 1–4cm long when fully extended. They are often found in damp areas such as rainforest and buttongrass, particularly during and after rain. Attaching themselves to the feet, ankle or lower leg, they make a small incision and use a compound in their saliva to allow the blood to flow while they feed. After feeding they drop off, the whole process so painless that many hikers only discover they've been bitten when they remove their shoes and socks and see blood. Some people have an allergic reaction to leech bites and should take an antihistamine.

In wet conditions tuck your socks into your pants and check your boots and legs regularly to pick off any leeches before they bite. If you discover one attached they can be induced to let go by persistent rubbing or else with the application of salt or tea-tree oil.

Mosquitoes

Mosquitoes are most abundant during summer when there's more stagnant water along the track. Cover up in the evenings and apply insect repellent.

Snakes

Tasmania has only three types of snake: the tiger, the white-lipped and the lowland copperhead. From colour alone they can be hard to tell apart – experts do so by counting their body scales.

All three species are venomous – the copperhead and tiger snake among the 10 most venomous in the world – although they are generally placid. There's never been a recorded death in Tasmania from the copperhead or the white-lipped snake, and the last fatality from a tiger snake was in 1966. Seriously, peanuts kill more people. The same anti-venom is effective for all three snakes.

Tasmanian snakes are often darker than their mainland counterparts, an adaptation to the cooler conditions. Being cold-blooded, snakes rely on the sun to raise their body temperature stretching out to warm up, then coiling themselves to maintain warmth. You may come across a snake sunning itself on the track. Great – they're amazing creatures. Snakes don't want a fight – they'll only strike if trapped or threatened. Stay still, or back away very slowly if safe to do so. Snakes are most active between October and March. In winter they hibernate in rodent burrows, hollow logs or tree stumps until conditions warm up in spring. Copperheads and tiger snakes may be active on warm nights so take a torch with you when walking. Surprisingly snakes are great swimmers, swimming faster than they travel on land, which is actually quite slow – about the speed of a nice brisk walk.

For more information on identifying these amazing creatures see the Plant and animal guide.

Jack jumper ants

Jack jumpers are small ants with a sting as painful as a bee's. Their black bodies are 10–15mm long with orange/brown pincers and legs. They're very aggressive when disturbed, moving in jerky jumps. While most people only experience local swelling (which can be minimised with antihistamines), 2–3 per cent of Tasmanians (who are more

HOW TO TREAT A SNAKEBITE

Keep the victim as still and calm as possible, as movement causes the poison to spread through the lymphatic system. First apply a pressure bandage over the bite site. Then apply a firm crepe or elasticised roller bandage, starting just above the fingers or toes (most bites occur on a limb) and moving to the top of the bitten appendage. If you don't have bandages, use clothing or another material. Immobilise the limb with a splint (such as a stick or walking pole), holding it in place with another bandage. Call 000 if you happen to have mobile coverage, or else activate a Personal Locator Beacon. If you don't have a distress beacon or can't get mobile reception, send two people to a hut for help, leaving at least one person with the victim. It is important the victim is kept as still as possible. Do not apply a tourniquet or cut and suck the snakebite. Don't attempt to catch the snake: in Tasmania the same snake anti-venom is effective for all bites.

likely to have been bitten before and developed an allergy) have a severe allergic reaction, which, at its most serious, can lead to life-threatening anaphylaxis. Jack jumper stings claimed four lives in the state between 1980 and 2000.

Fortunately, the fine gravel mound that often surrounds ant nests makes them possible to identify and avoid, and as the ants prefer relatively dry areas they are not overly abundant on the Overland.

Hikers known to have severe allergic reactions to insect stings, such as bees or wasps, should carry an adrenaline EpiPen in their first aid kits.

Other hassles and dangers

Sunburn

The thin ozone layer over Tasmania means the sun strikes with particular ferocity and UV radiation is high. Bring sunscreen, a broad-rimmed hat and a long-sleeved shirt.

Hypothermia

Hypothermia occurs when the body can't warm itself sufficiently, a condition exacerbated by wet clothes, wind, fatigue and hunger. Early symptoms can include clumsiness and shivering, and pale, cold skin, and if not treated can lead to slurred speech, irrational behaviour, unconsciousness and death. In 2014 a hiker died of hypothermia on the Overland – in summer.

The best way to prevent hypothermia is to avoid exposure – bring appropriate, good quality clothing and stay dry. See Appendix B 'Suggested clothing, gear and food'.

If hypothermia is detected in a member of your party, stop hiking and treat immediately. If possible, get the victim out of the wind and rain by setting up a tent, get them in dry clothing and into a sleeping bag. Warm, sweet drinks and a heat donor to share the sleeping bag can help restore body heat.

Blisters

Blisters are one of the most common causes of track misery. Make sure your boots fit and wear them in before embarking on the Overland. Tape up 'hotspots' before they become blisters.

Rooty track heading towards Pelion Gap (Stage 4)

Track surface

Slippery roots, awkward rocks, deep mud and icy duckboards (parallel boards laid over muddy ground) provide plenty of opportunity for slipping over. Hiking boots with good grip and ankle support will minimise falls and twisted ankles. Many Overlanders use hiking poles to maintain their footing and reduce knee-strain.

Gastroenteritis

Gastro can cause diarrhoea, vomiting and abdominal cramps. It can be avoided by purifying drinking water or by boiling it for three minutes. Chances of suffering the illness can be minimised by only collecting drinking water from huts' rainwater tanks, or from water flowing upstream from the track in areas unlikely to have been used as rest stops (as people have often gone to the toilet in the vicinity of these areas).

Minimise the risk of gastro by washing your hands after going to the toilet and before eating (use liquid hand-sanitiser if water is not available), and by cleaning hut benches before preparing food.

If gastro strikes, drink plenty of fluids to avoid dehydration and be mindful of hygiene to avoid spreading the condition. Gastro-stop capsules, or similar diarrhoea treatment, can help you continue hiking.

PHONES AND WI-FI

While most people are only too delighted to be out of contact with the rest of the world, many still carry a mobile phone on the Overland in case of emergency or to get updated weather forecasts. Although Tasmania wasn't formed with good mobile phone reception in mind, there are still a few places along the track where reception may be possible, particularly on the Telstra network. Some places worth trying include Cradle Mountain Hotel, Marions Lookout, near Kitchen Hut, near Lake Will, the River Forth Lookout, the helipad near Pine Valley Hut, on the jetty near Narcissus Hut, Echo Point jetty and Cynthia Bay, as well as on peaks such as Cradle Mountain, Mt Oakleigh, Mt Ossa and Mt Pelion East.

Thirty minutes of free Wi-Fi is available at the Cradle Mountain Visitor Centre. Wi-Fi is also available at most of Cradle Valley's eateries and hotels.

At Cynthia Bay Wi-Fi is available at the Lake St Clair Visitor Centre.

THE OVERLAND TRACK

The sinuous boardwalk leading towards Narcissus Hut with Mt Olympus in the background (Stage 6)

STAGE 1

Ronny Creek to Waterfall Valley Huts

Start	Ronny Creek (Cradle Valley)
Alternative start	Dove Lake car park
Finish	Waterfall Valley Huts
Distance	11.0km
Total ascent	565m
Total descent	405m
Grade	Medium–hard
Time	3½–5½hr
Maximum altitude	1271m
Possible sidetrips	Cradle Mountain (medium–hard); Barn Bluff (medium–hard)

The first day is the most difficult, with exposed sections and a tough climb to Marions Lookout. There's much to admire on the way though, including patches of rainforest, stunning lakes and incredible alpine meadows. Kitchen Hut, a wooden hut weathered grey by the elements, is a good place for lunch or a break. An alternative is to start the hike at Dove Lake instead of Ronny Creek. This allows you to enjoy the classic view of Cradle Mountain across the lake before rejoining the main Overland Track (see Alternative start). For more information on transfers between Cradle Valley and Ronny Creek, see the introduction to this guide, 'Accommodation and facilities at the start of the track'.

Note: the Waterfall Valley Huts will be closed from November 2019 to May 2020 while a new hut is constructed. During construction hikers need to stay at the Scott-Kilvert Memorial Hut, a 2.1km diversion from the main Overland Track route. Staying at the Scott-Kilvert Memorial Hut makes Stage 1 10.6km instead of 11.0km. Stage 2 to Windermere Hut increases from 7.7km to 12.3km.

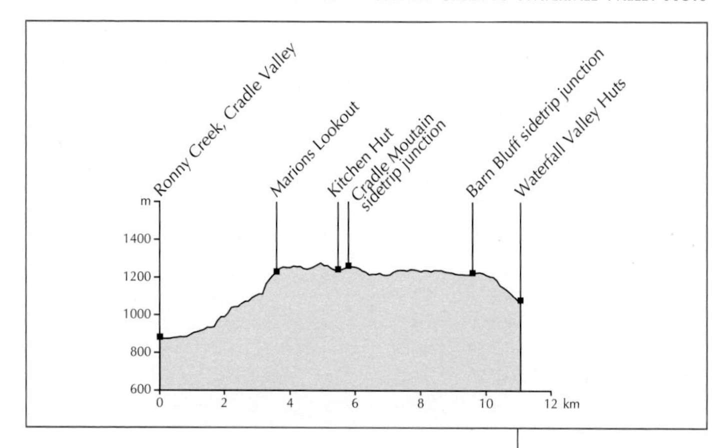

Ronny Creek Car Park to Kitchen Hut, 5.5km, 2–3hr

Sign in at the walkers' registration booth at Ronny Creek and then start the track, following the boardwalk that meanders along the broad, grassy Cradle Valley. The valley is etched with small streams and pools, the track passing banks of alpine coralfern and scattered pandani. Note the lone boulder about 150m from the start of the walk, a glacial erratic (a rock carried and then deposited by the glacier that carved Cradle Valley). ▸

The valley is also a good place to spot wombats, especially in overcast weather.

After 750m, cross **Ronny Creek** on a bridge and follow the arrows for the Overland past the track to Wombat Pool. The path rises through swathes of buttongrass into eucalypt forest with a lovely section beside **Crater Creek** as you arrive at the junction with **Horse Track** (so named because the route allowed packhorses – which supported early hikers – access to Cradle Plateau). Continue straight, crossing Crater Creek, to begin the long steady climb towards Crater Lake on a path of pale, crushed rock.

Enter dense, mossy rainforest, where a series of cascades leads to **Crater Falls** tumbling among the sassafras and myrtle beech. Stairs climb out of the gully past deciduous beech and back into moorland, with views ahead to the formidable bluff below **Marions Lookout**.

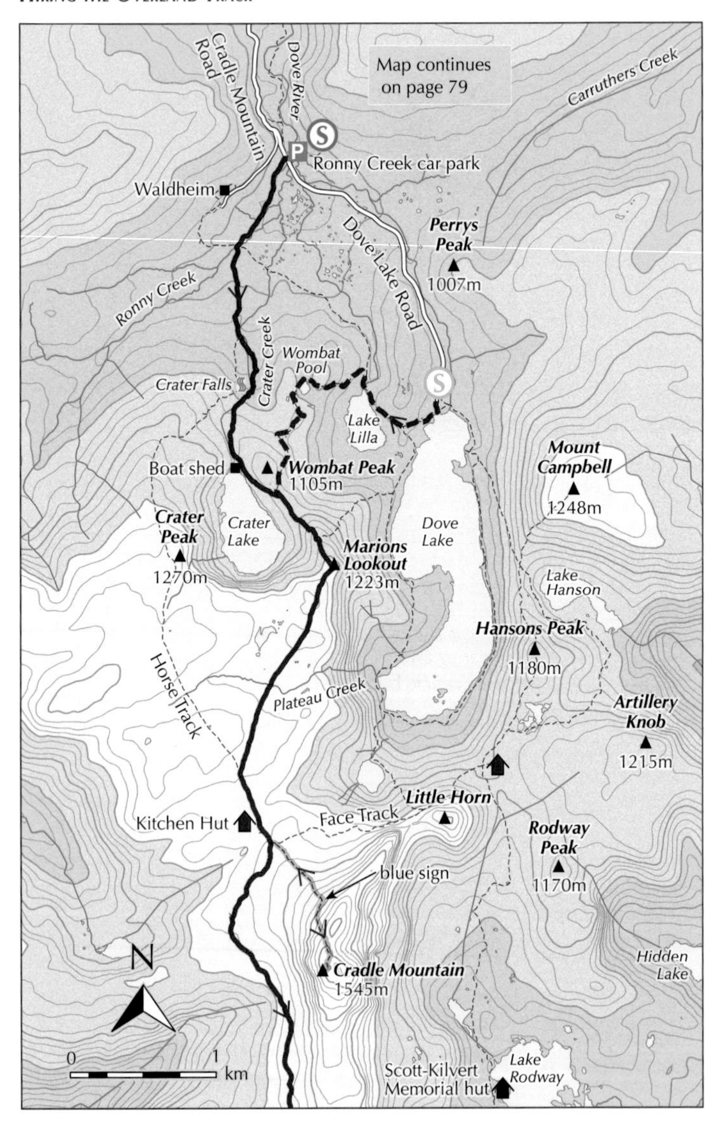
Map continues
on page 79
Cradle Mountain
Road
Dove River
Carruthers Creek
Ronny Creek car park
Waldheim
Perrys
Peak
1007m
Dove Lake Road
Ronny Creek
Crater Creek
Wombat
Pool
Crater Falls
Lake
Lilla
Mount
Campbell
1248m
Boat shed
Wombat Peak
1105m
Crater
Peak
1270m
Crater
Lake
Dove
Lake
Marions
Lookout
1223m
Lake
Hanson
Hansons Peak
1180m
Horse Track
Plateau Creek
Artillery
Knob
1215m
Little Horn
Kitchen Hut
Face Track
Rodway
Peak
1170m
blue sign
Hidden
Lake
N
Cradle Mountain
1545m
0
1
km
Scott-Kilvert
Memorial hut
Lake
Rodway

The boatshed at Crater Lake

The **boat shed** at **Crater Lake** is reached, a spectacularly weathered shingle hut with wonderful views across the lake. ▶

From late April into May, this is a great place to admire the autumnal colours of the surrounding deciduous beech.

Crater Lake is a good example of a cirque (see 'Geology' section), where a glacier has formed in the lee of a mountain, wearing away a deep hole that subsequently filled with water to become a lake.

The track skirts around the eastern side of the lake, the shore fringed with King Billy pines, then climbs to reach an exposed ridge and the junction with the alternative start via Dove Lake and Wombat Pool, 2.8km from Ronny Creek. ▶

There's a wooden platform with good views over Dove Lake and the smaller Lake Lilla.

Alternative start from Dove Lake car park (via Lake Lilla and Wombat Pool)

2.5km, 45min. Ascent/descent: 190m/50m.

This alternative start rejoins the track near the base of Marions Lookout and takes in the breathtaking view of Cradle Mountain across Dove Lake and Wombat Pool. Although slightly shorter than the route from Ronny Creek, it involves a steeper climb.

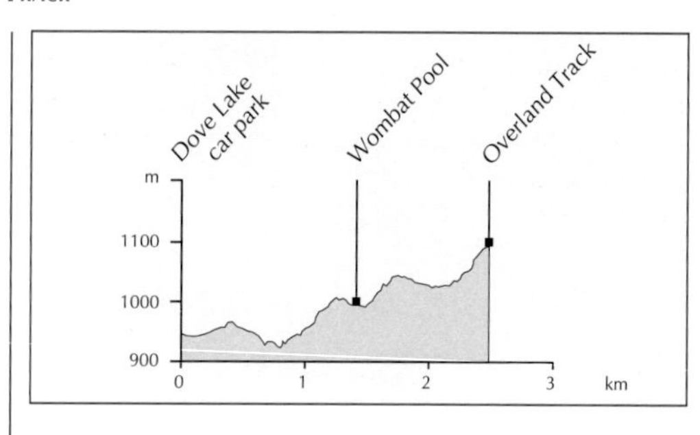

After enjoying the view of the ragged tooth of **Cradle Mountain** across Dove Lake, follow the 'Ronny Ck via Lake Lilla' sign to the south-west, climbing slightly to reach a junction with the Dove Lake circuit track after 350m. Continue straight, **Lake Lilla** coming into view to the left before entering the shade and shelter of rainforest, rock steps leading down to Lilla Creek, with the lake nestled beautifully between the hills.

Cross the creek to reach a track junction after 50m. Turn left and begin the short, steep climb to **Wombat Pool**, a small circular lake fringed with ancient, bleached pencil pines.

From Wombat Pool the junction with the Overland is 1.1km away. Climb steeply again to a lookout 20m off the main track with views over Dove Lake, Lake Lilla and down Cradle Valley. A further steady slog takes you towards **Wombat Peak**, the smooth round hill ahead. The track joins the Overland near Crater Lake, the bluff of Marions Lookout just ahead.

From the junction with the alternative start via Lake Lilla and Wombat Pool, head south towards Marions Lookout. The climb begins with rock-strewn steps, stunted snow peppermints and deciduous beech growing in the meagre shelter of the escarpment. The steps climb, slowly becoming steeper, until towards the top of the first peak there's a chain-rope to help haul yourself up the rock face. ◂

If you've brought too much gear this is where you'll realise your mistake.

After the first peak the track levels off to a steady climb following the ridge to a junction of a trail descending to **Dove Lake**. Continue along the ridge for 250m – metal marker-poles indicating the route in dense fog or snow – until reaching a track junction near **Marions Lookout**. The lookout, 20m from the junction, has superb views over Dove Lake.

The **movement of ice** during the ice age scoured Marions Lookout and Cradle Plateau flat, while the surrounding peaks like Cradle Mountain and Barn Bluff were above the level of the abrading ice.

From the lookout continue up a final rise to reach Cradle Plateau – the most difficult climb on the track is now over. The track enters alpine communities studded with small, clear pools, cushionplants and creeping pine. ▶

The plants grow low to the ground to avoid the worst of the wind, with special adaptations like small leaves and tough stems to help them survive the extreme conditions.

About 1km from Marions Lookout descend into a shallow gully to cross **Plateau Creek** on a bridge, its clear waters trickling over white rocks. At 1271m, the ridge above the gully is the highest point on the Overland's main track.

Follow the boardwalk as it snakes down towards **Kitchen Hut**, ending near a junction with **Horse Track**, 1.6km from Marions Lookout. Neat paving and more boardwalk takes you the remaining 400m to the hut. Past Kitchen Hut the track becomes less frequented as it's beyond the range of most day-trippers.

KITCHEN HUT

Kitchen Hut is a tiny two-level shingle building built on a raised rock platform, strengthened against the often ferocious winds by steel cables. A spade high up on the outside wall gives an indication of how much snow can sometimes fall in this area. The hut makes a great place for a break with a small table and bench inside, and the possibility of seeing one of the eastern quolls that frequent the area. It also makes a good place to leave your pack if doing the Cradle Mountain sidetrip, as the sidetrip junction is only 150m further south along the Overland. There's a toilet 80m south of the hut, just to the right of the track.

Sidetrip: Cradle Mountain

2.6km, 2½–3½hr return. Total ascent/descent: 355m return. Grade: Medium–hard.

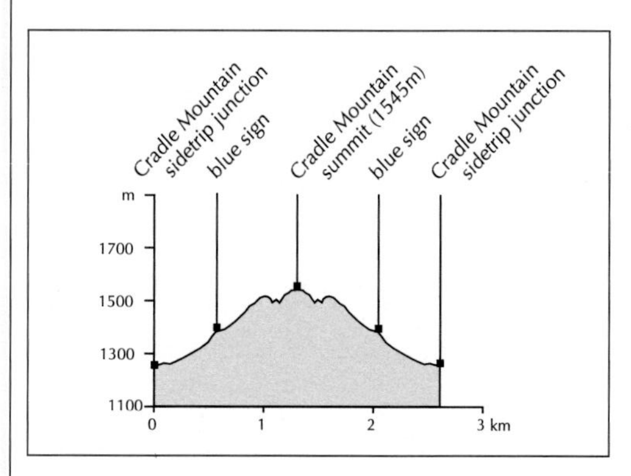

This is a steep, sometimes difficult climb requiring free hands to scramble over boulders towards the summit. While helicopter tours of Cradle Valley are available, those climbing Cradle Mountain (1545m) won't need to take one – the view from the top is one of the highlights of the walk.

The Cradle Mountain sidetrip begins 150m southeast of Kitchen Hut along a trail marked **Face Track**. Follow this track for 30m to reach a second junction. Turn right, following the sign to **Cradle Mountain** summit.

Initially the path is a well-defined, deeply furrowed, rocky track marked with white poles. The track soon gets steeper, scree turning to jumbled stones and larger rocks. About 550m from the last junction reach a blue sign indicating the route to Cradle Mountain summit. As the track continues to climb the rocks give way to boulders spotted with impressive collections of coloured lichens.

Picking your way through the boulders, the white pole markers become essential for following the track, the boulder-hopping becoming hand-over-hand climbing, with a few tricky sections that require great care.

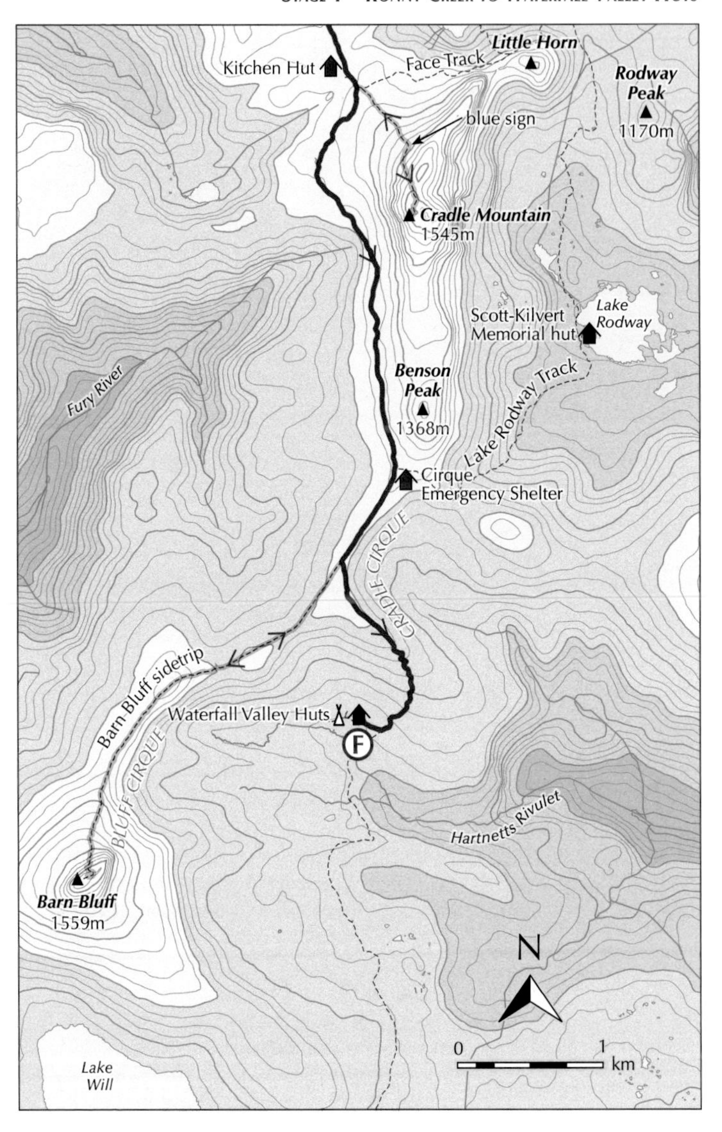
Little Horn
Kitchen Hut
Face Track
Rodway Peak
1170m
blue sign
Cradle Mountain
1545m
Lake Rodway
Scott-Kilvert Memorial hut
Benson Peak
1368m
Fury River
Lake Rodway Track
Cirque Emergency Shelter
CRADLE CIRQUE
Barn Bluff sidetrip
Waterfall Valley Huts
F
BLUFF CIRQUE
Hartnetts Rivulet
Barn Bluff
1559m
N
0
1
km
Lake Will

The route up Cradle Mountain is steep but well worth the effort on a fine day

The view from the top makes the excursion worthwhile: a panorama with Barn Bluff to the south-west and Kitchen Hut far below.

A steep scramble leads to a saddle between huge dolerite columns. The track dips down, the strap leaves of the lily-like silky milligania growing in profusion, before a short, final scramble up and over the boulders to the summit. ◂ The Overland Track is visible as a fine white line etched into the landscape.

It was from the summit of Cradle Mountain in 1910 that **Gustav Weindorfer** declared, 'This must be a national park for the people for all time. It is magnificent, and people must know about it and enjoy it'. The brass direction plate on the summit was designed by Weindorfer to commemorate surveyor Henry Hellyer climbing the mountain in 1831, Cradle's first officially recorded ascent.

Retrace your steps to rejoin the Overland Track.

Kitchen Hut to Waterfall Valley Huts, 5.5km, 1½–2½hr

From Kitchen Hut pass the Cradle Mountain **sidetrip turn-off** after 150m (marked 'Face Track'), climbing slightly as the blunt rock nub of **Barn Bluff** appears ahead. The track continues across the alpine vegetation of the plateau, which includes cushionplants, pineapple grass and deciduous beech. Passing several idyllic tarns, Cradle Mountain's fractured columnar flank rears up to the east, before the track enters snow peppermint forest – the eucalypt most tolerant of Tasmania's harsh, high altitude conditions.

This **forest**, like many along the track, is littered with the bleached trunks of dead trees. These trunks are often the remains of pencil and King Billy pines killed by fire. In the last century alone, a third of the King Billy pine population has succumbed to flames.

The walking becomes slower as the track becomes a mix of rocks and mud, the jumbled hillside of **Benson Peak** appearing to the south-east. At the junction with the **Lake Rodway Track** (which leads to the **Scott-Kilvert Memorial Hut**, 2.1km way, named after the teacher and student who died of hypothermia in the area in 1965), you can see the distant chain of mountains stretching away to the south-east, the Overland passing between many of them on its way south. From here Waterfall Valley Huts are 2.5km.

Just after the junction, to the left of the track, is a bulbous green plastic pod known as the **Cirque Emergency Shelter**, looking eerily like a spacecraft. The shelter was installed in 2017, three years after a man died from exposure nearby.

Soon after you pass the emergency shelter the walking becomes easier as the track follows the gentle, curved rim of **Cradle Cirque**, with breathtaking views east to the bald double knob of Mt Emmett and the Forth River Valley beyond. ▶

The track is lined with wind-pruned shrubs, an indication of how exposed this section is to wild weather.

Around 750m from the Lake Rodway Track junction, reach the **junction** with the Barn Bluff sidetrip and continue along Cradle Cirque, duckboards and boardwalks making for easy hiking until the track begins to descend into Waterfall Valley.

Descend steeply along switchbacks through scoparia and pandani, before arriving at a junction near the huts. A boardwalk leads off the main track to the huts, which are 160m east at the edge of the forest beside the plain – a beautiful setting.

WATERFALL VALLEY HUTS

There are two Waterfall Valley Huts, a larger one, located closer to the main track, which sleeps 24, and a smaller hut, 100m further on, a more basic affair which sleeps four. The larger hut is due to be knocked down and replaced by a better insulated 34-person shelter, scheduled for completion in May 2020. There are two toilets, a newer one near the main hut and an older one nearer the camping area. The campsites are on the grass near the old hut, with those further down the slope becoming quite damp. The group campsite is up the track behind the old hut.

A loud, cranky Tasmanian native hen often patrols the campsite and around the huts. Wombats are also common. Be sure to check out the beautiful waterfall behind the old hut. As with all overnight stays, make sure you keep your food and rubbish hung up inside a hut so the critters don't scoff the lot.

Sidetrip: **Barn Bluff**

6.2km, 3–4hr return. Total ascent/descent: 480m return. Grade: Medium–hard.

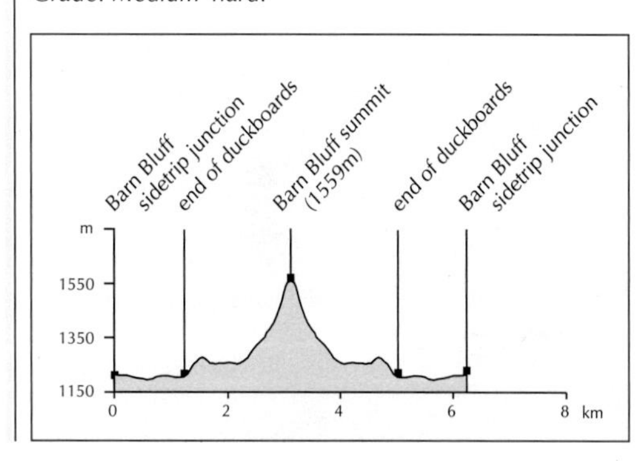

Barn Bluff is one of the lesser climbed mountains on the track, which gives this sidetrip a bit of an intrepid feeling. The view from the top rivals Cradle Mountain, as it should – Barn Bluff, at 1559m, is 14m higher and Tassie's fourth highest mountain. ▶ Most of the hike is fairly level as it rounds Bluff Cirque, but the climb is very steep in places, requiring the use of both hands to clamber over boulders. Some sections can be muddy and slippery after rain. The route up the mountain is marked only with small cairns, so good visibility is vital.

The sidetrip can be done on the first day, or on the second if hikers backtrack 1.7km from Waterfall Valley Huts to the junction.

From the junction, duckboards lead smoothly along a ridge of low alpine vegetation, including cushionplants, central lemon boronia and mountain rocket. Ahead the fractured face of the bluff seems insurmountable, the path up its northern side invisible.

After 1.2km the track leaves the duckboards and climbs a short, steep hill, then descends to follow the edge of **Bluff Cirque**, the views already superb. The cirque leads to the base of the bluff, the sides of the mountain littered with boulders cleaved from above by the splitting action of ice freezing and thawing in cracks.

Now the climb really begins. The rocky path initially rises gently, the bluff's spires beginning to loom overhead.

Cradle Cirque, on the way to the Waterfall Valley Huts, can be exposed to bad weather

The stones gradually grow larger until the track picks its way through beautiful lichen-spotted boulders near the base of the dolerite cliffs. The track here becomes indistinct, marked only with small cairns leading up towards a break in the boulders between the columns above. There are a few tricky sections, and some scrambling up loose banks of scree. Towards the top the track branches into two; take the left turn as the route to the right soon peters out.

And then you are at the top, and, on a clear day, the king or queen of the national park. ◄ Beyond the lake the entire plateau is studded with smaller pools until you reach the bulk of Mt Pelion West. Looking north, the track just climbed appears as a chalk line tapering back to the shaggy head of Cradle Mountain. On a good day the track is visible far beyond, skirting all the way back towards Marions Lookout. Barn Bluff is well worth the effort.

The 360° view is like an aerial map of the northern section of the walk, with Lake Will to the south, just below the jut of the bluff, its white beaches appealing on a warm day.

Return the way you came and rejoin the Overland Track.

Barn Bluff from the junction with the main track

STAGE 2

Waterfall Valley Huts to Windermere Hut

Start	Waterfall Valley Huts
Finish	Windermere Hut
Distance	7.7km
Total ascent	200m
Total descent	230m
Grade	Easy–medium
Time	2–3hr
Maximum altitude	1112m
Possible sidetrips	Lake Will Beach (easy)

A relatively short, level day over exposed buttongrass and heath plains. Lakes are the feature of today, including a chance to visit Lake Will and a walk around the shore of the beautiful, island-studded Lake Windermere.

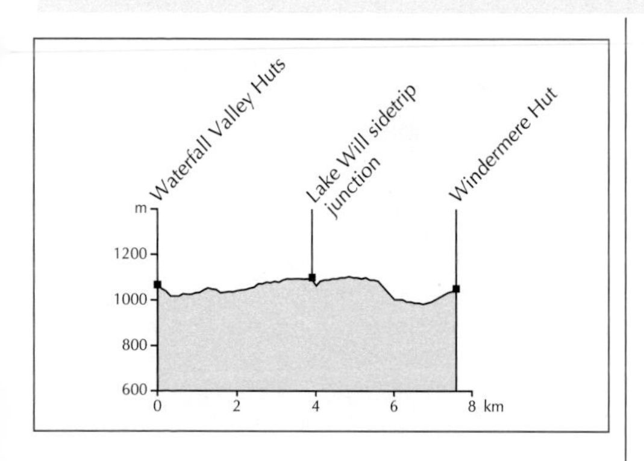

Waterfall Valley Huts to Lake Will sidetrip junction, 3.8km, 1–1½hr

From the main track near Waterfall Valley Huts the Overland gently descends to cross the plain, buttongrass returning as the track climbs again to a level, rocky path on the edge of Waterfall Valley. After 1.1km the track

Lake Will and associates. The view from Barn Bluff

turns sharply west to follow the ridgeline on a boardwalk before curving around south-east again, descending steeply into the next valley through pines and deciduous beech then entering a marshy area where alpine and moorland species mix.

Climbing the next ridge, there are views north-east to the vast pile of scree that is Mt Emmett. The track levels out as it follows duckboards through cider gum woodland around the buttress that supports Barn Bluff, **Lake Holmes** soon appearing to the south-east, the huge plain of moorland ahead stretching south far out of sight.

If you're leaving your pack for the sidetrip put on a pack cover – the currawongs around here have worked out how to open zips!

The track approaches Lake Holmes 3.8km from Waterfall Valley Huts and the junction for the sidetrip to Lake Will. A raised wooden platform by the junction makes a good place for a break. ◂

Sidetrip: Lake Will Beach

3.2km, 1¼hr return. Total ascent/descent: 50m return. Grade: Easy.

This is an easy amble over duckboards to a picturesque lake, Lake Will, with a sandy beach lined with pencil pines.

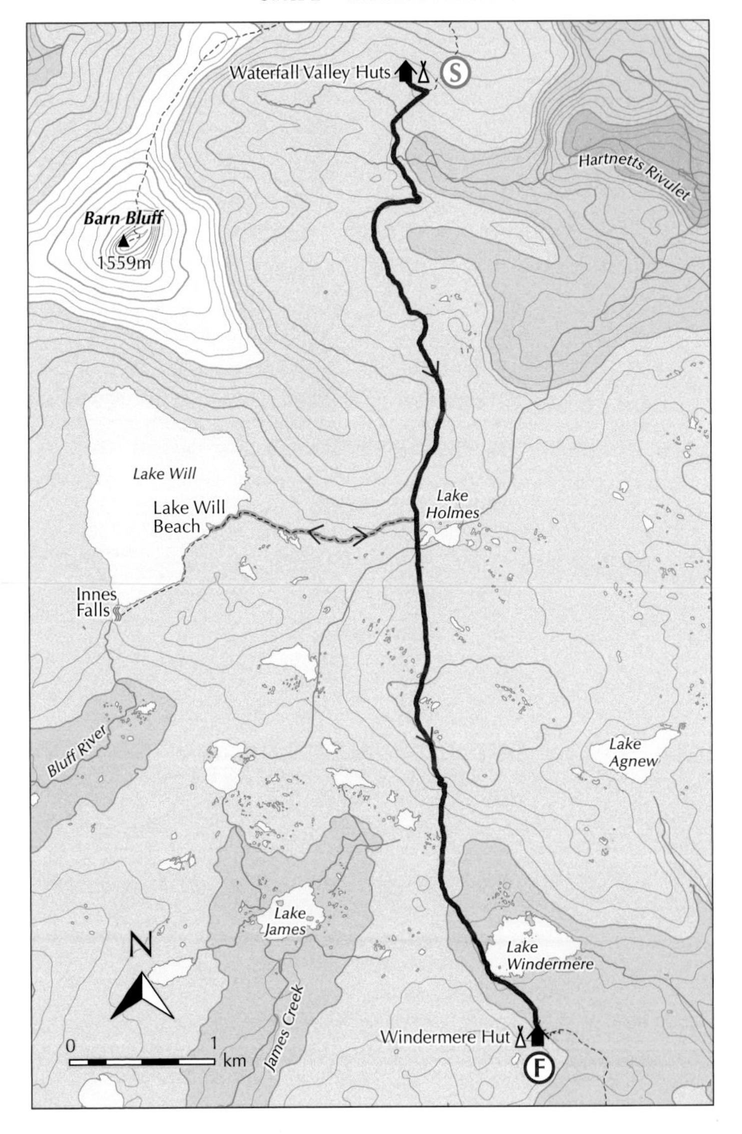
Waterfall Valley Huts
S
Hartnetts Rivulet
Barn Bluff
1559m
Lake Will
Lake Will
Beach
Lake
Holmes
Innes
Falls
Bluff River
Lake
Agnew
Lake
James
Lake
Windermere
N
0
1
km
James Creek
Windermere Hut
F

Duckboards lead west through southern cordrush, boronia species and alpine coralfern, crossing several mounds of coal – remains of the deposit worked by Joseph Will in 1893, from whom the lake gets its name. The duckboards lead all the way to the lake, crossing peaty soil through dense stands of scoparia.

Lake Will is first glimpsed to the south-west, with the impressive bulk of **Barn Bluff** to the north. The duckboards lead past a long, thin tarn and then gradually down to a little white quartzite sand beach fringed with gnarled pencil pines. Crossing the beach, continue along the lake shore for another 230m to a second, larger beach which makes a lovely place to lounge in warm weather. The track continues along the lake edge to **Innes Falls** near the southern rim of the lake, another 2km, 1 hour return. As the track to the falls is muddy and the 4m falls are not particularly spectacular, it's only recommended for waterfall enthusiasts.

Retrace your steps and rejoin the Overland Track.

Lake Will sidetrip junction to Windermere Hut, 3.9km, 1–1½hr

From the junction with the Lake Will sidetrip the track continues past a sign for Lake Holmes, the boardwalk zig-zagging across the plain through southern cordrush, alpine coralfern and broadleaf boronia towards the ridge to the south. Near the ridge, an eroded white rock path leads over the rise revealing the mountains ahead, Mt Pelion West prominent at the edge of the plain. Duckboards descend past outcrops of white and grey quartzite, the lake-dotted plain to the east containing lakes Agnew, McRae and Ellen, Cradle Mountain and Barn Bluff still visible to the north.

The track descends past a rocky knoll of gums 1.8km from the Lake Will turn-off, with brilliant views over **Lake Windermere** and its scattering of islands.

A paved track descends through myrtle beech, deciduous beech and mountain geebung towards the lake, the path levelling off across a buttongrass plain. The track winds down to the edge of the lake through a varied mix

Lake Windermere

of vegetation, the path lined with rocks tinted an intense red by lichen. Following the lakeside, reach a sign, 'No camping within 50m of the lake'. Nearby is a lakeside rest and swimming area with logs and stone paving.The hut is now only 560m away.

The track turns away from the lake and up a slight rise past a huge pencil pine and an equally large snow peppermint. **Windermere Hut** is tucked among the tall, lush myrtle beeches and woolly tea-trees.

WINDERMERE HUT

Windermere Hut offers glimpses of the lake from the hut's veranda. The hut sleeps 16 and has separate dining and sleeping rooms. There are nine camping platforms scattered about the edge of the forest, some quite private. The wildlife here is abundant and accustomed to hikers: in the evening it's a great place to see wombats, possums, pademelons and Bennett's wallabies. The brushtail possums here are huge and bold.

STAGE 3

Windermere Hut to New Pelion Hut

Start	Windermere Hut
Finish	New Pelion Hut
Distance	15.3km
Total ascent	520m
Total descent	665m
Grade	Medium
Time	5–6½hr
Maximum altitude	1028m
Possible sidetrips	River Forth Lookout (easy); Old Pelion Hut (easy); Mt Oakleigh (medium)

Allow plenty of time for today's walk as the second half of the hike is partly through thick myrtle rainforest, where the path becomes rocky, muddy and tangled with roots.

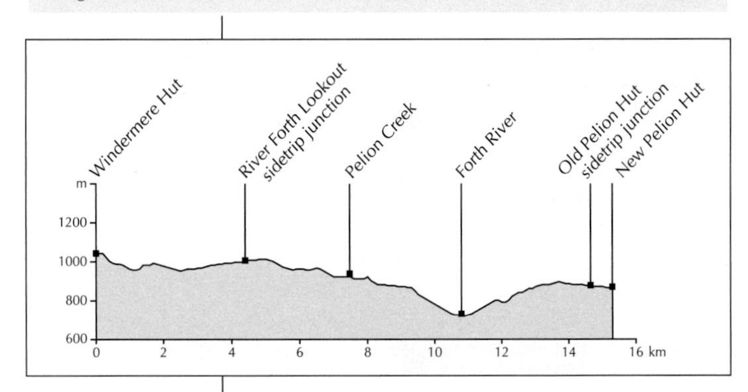

Windermere Hut to Pelion Creek, 7.4km, 2½–3hr

From Windermere Hut the track continues through open snow peppermint woodland. The path descends into dense myrtle beech and woolly tea-tree before emerging to views of **Lake Curran** to the south-west and the vast Forth River Valley to the east.

A boardwalk continues over a scoparia-studded plain, crossing **Curran Creek**, then steadily climbing a jumbled rock path through buttongrass to reach the top of the ridge. The rocky track continues, descending to the south-east, with the bulwarks of **Mt Pelion West** ahead. The track levels off across a plain, the path briefly fringed with shiny tea-tree before descending into the shelter of woolly tea-tree and myrtle beech again, the rainforest creating a hushed, magical atmosphere.

The rainforest ends abruptly 2.4km from Windermere Hut at a boardwalk carved with 'Pine Forest Moor' (misleading as Pine Forest Moor isn't a specific location, as some maps indicate, but the entire plain between Windermere Hut and Mt Pelion West).

Muddy track through the rainforest near Pelion Creek

Map continues on page 95

Steps climb the next ridge to a wide, exposed, buttongrass plain with a panorama of the surrounding mountains. Duckboards gently descend over an outcrop of conglomerate rock to a narrow strip of land between two valleys, continuing south-east over the plain towards the forested hill ahead.

Just before the track enters the forest, 4.2km from Windermere Hut, there's a junction with a side track to the **River Forth Lookout** with logs for sitting or resting your pack.

Sidetrip: **River Forth Lookout**

130m, 10min return. Total ascent/descent: 10m return. Grade: Easy.

The stone benches at the lookout make a good place for a break with the chance to see a wedge-tailed eagle.

The lookout is 65m along the side track, on the edge of the immense, glacier-carved valley, with Mt Oakleigh on the far side. This idyllic scene could have looked much different: the Lemonthyme Forest below was only saved from logging by a last-ditch stand by conservationists in 1986.

Return to the main trail.

From the junction with the lookout, a tangle of boulders, roots and mud leads into the forested area. The moss-covered boulders and myrtle trunks create a peaceful ambiance as the track climbs, passing the occasional celerytop pine before descending through giant pandani and scattered Tasmanian waratahs, to suddenly emerge at a boardwalk across a buttongrass plain. A small track leads 250m east to a private hut.

Mt Pelion West is now close enough to reveal its fractured face of dolerite columns to the south, while on a clear day New Pelion Hut is visible in a clearing far to the south-east. This section of track to Pelion Plains is part of the **Innes Track**, cut by Surveyor Edward Innes in 1896–1897 to link the area with Rosebery, a mining settlement on the west coast.

Cross a pencil pine-lined creek on a bridge, the track heading south-east over the plain towards the wooded lower slopes of Mt Pelion West. Drop into a gully to cross a second bridge before duckboards descend to a third bridge over a creek at the edge of the forest. **Pelion Creek** is about 600m further into the diverse wet eucalypt forest, a substantial creek and bridge, with a wooden platform that makes a good place for a break, 3.2km from the River Forth Lookout, 7.4km from Windermere Hut.

Pelion Creek to New Pelion Hut, 7.9km, 2½–3½hr

The track through myrtle rainforest to Frog Flats is a mix of mud, boulders, puddles and roots, making hiking slow. After 700m cross a landslip to enter rainforest dominated by leatherwood, the track becoming lined with huge clumps of strap-leaved cutting grass. ◄ The track gradually descends past several streams until finally arriving in the damp, leechy area known as **Frog Flats**.

A change to a slightly drier aspect encourages a more open forest with celerytop pine, silver banksia and gumtopped stringybarks becoming more common.

NOT SEEING THE FOREST FOR THE WOODCHIPS

Tasmania has long been a battleground between those who wish to exploit the island's forests and those who wish to preserve them. In 1986 this battle was fought near Cradle Mountain, in the Lemonthyme Forest, when logging machinery moved in to clearfell the area. By blockading the road protestors managed to keep out the loggers until a federal government inquiry determined that the area was worthy of inclusion in an expanded world heritage area. One of the crucial arguments used to protect the forest was the desecration of the view of the Forth River Valley from the Overland Track.

Unfortunately not all areas are so publicly visible. Today clearfelling of Tasmania's old-growth forests continues in areas adjoining the world heritage area. One current flash-point is the Tarkine in north-west Tasmania, a globally significant wilderness area containing large swathes of pristine cool temperate rainforest. For more information visit www.wilderness.org.au.

Out of the dark rainforest the track continues its slow descent over a buttongrass field before re-entering rainforest to reach the **Forth River**, 3.6km from Pelion

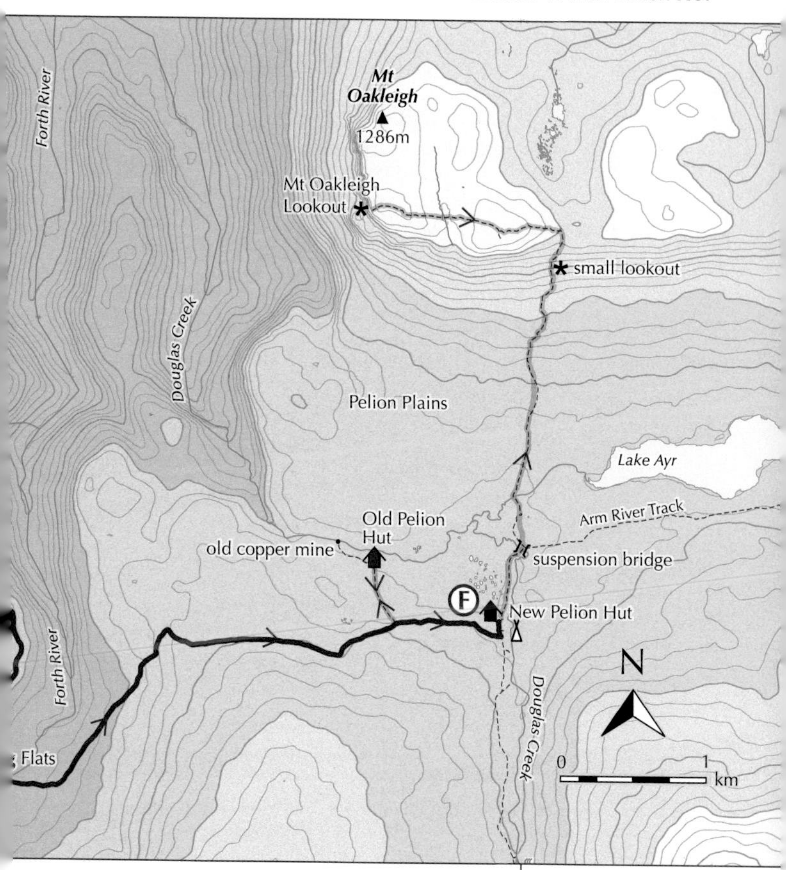

Creek, the river that inhabits the huge valley viewed earlier from the lookout. At 718m, this is the lowest point on the Overland. ▸

Leaving the river, duckboards lead over a tussock grass field with a good view south to the escarpment of Mt Doris, beside Mt Ossa, before returning to myrtle rainforest, whose green mossy depths are crossed by a series of streams.

This is a lovely sheltered spot for a break, with log seats among the towering myrtle beech and snow peppermint.

Begin a long, gradual climb, the vegetation becoming drier, eucalypts replacing the rainforest, mountain pinkberry becoming common. A short section of black mesh boardwalk heralds the top of the main climb, the last before New Pelion Hut, 2.1km away.

Descend through a succession of buttongrass, myrtle beech and woodland, until the view opens onto the vast buttongrass and grassland field of Pelion Plains, Mt Oakleigh on their far side, its individual rock spires revealed. The **junction** with the track to Old Pelion Hut is soon reached.

Sidetrip: **Old Pelion Hut**

880m, 30min return. Total ascent/descent: 30m return. Grade: Easy.

A short walk to the oldest hut in the national park, with the beautiful Douglas Creek nearby. Bring a head torch if you want to extend the walk by 330m (each way) and explore an old copper mine.

The track starts at the edge of the grassy plain and continues through a fringe of eucalypts, **Mt Oakleigh** rearing up and tapering away to the east. The track descends through buttongrass and woodland, duckboards and boardwalk sparing you from the worst of the mud, before the corrugated-iron roof of the hut comes into view below.

OLD PELION HUT

The wooden planks of Old Pelion Hut are weathered white, the worn timberwork inside carved with countless names and dates stretching back to the 1920s. The hut, constructed in 1917, is one of the few remaining buildings predating the declaration of the national park in 1922. While minerals were first discovered on the Pelion Plains as far back as 1891, it wasn't until the World War I – and a boom in copper demand – that a serious attempt at extracting this potential mineral wealth was made.

In 1916 The Mount Pelion Mines No Liability Company was formed, constructing two huts on the plain in early 1917; one for the mine manager (Old Pelion Hut) and a second for the mine workers. When the copper content of the deposits proved too low to be viable, the company shifted their efforts to exploiting wolfram (tungsten) deposits on the slopes of Mt Oakleigh. In 1921 the company abandoned the site, and in 1922 transferred the ownership of the huts to the newly formed Cradle Mountain Reserves. Throughout the 1920s and '30s the buildings sheltered cattlemen who grazed their stock on the plains over summer, as well as increasing numbers of walkers, often guided by Paddy Hartnett or Bert Nichols. Cattle grazing continued on the Pelion Plains into the 1950s.

In around 1936 the workers' hut collapsed or was demolished. To avoid the same fate for Old Pelion Hut, in April 1936 Lionel Connell and his sons repaired and refurbished the building, particularly the interior. Their rough bush architecture, built to last, makes it a good place to sit and ponder.

In 2017 substantial repairs were made to the hut so it could celebrate its centenary in style. Old Pelion Hut is an emergency shelter only; overnight stays are not permitted.

There's a swimming hole in the Douglas Creek below the hut. Follow the sign marked 'water' 70m to the creek. Just downstream from the old bridge there's a deep pool that's magic for a swim when the weather's warm enough.

Also worth exploring is the sometimes rocky, sometimes muddy track heading north-west from the back of the hut. The track leads 330m to an **old copper mine** beside the creek marked with a mound of orange spoil. The mine – a head-high cave – extends about 50m into the hillside. Bring a head torch.

Retrace your steps to return to the Overland Track.

From the junction with the sidetrip to Old Pelion Hut the new hut is 900m away. The path continues through a mix of eucalypts at the edge of the plain, **New Pelion Hut** becoming visible through their smooth trunks. The hut is 100m off the main track at the edge of the plain.

NEW PELION HUT

New Pelion Hut, built in 2001, is a substantial building with four bunkrooms accommodating 36 (although there's actually room for 60 if people share the wider bunks). The hut can get busy at weekends and holidays when locals hike in 12km along the Arm River Track from a road at the edge of the park. There are camping platforms just south of the hut, as well as a selection of grassy campsites.

New Pelion has a large dining area with six tables, but its best feature is the veranda, which faces north across the Pelion Plains with a stunning view of Mt Oakleigh. Morning or evening, the veranda is a peaceful place to sit with a cup of tea or a book. Birds and other animals can be spotted close to the hut. The grassy plain is a good place to see animals in the evening or early morning.

Time permitting, New Pelion Hut makes the perfect place for a rest day, with the option of climbing Mt Oakleigh, visiting Old Pelion Hut or just hanging out on the veranda.

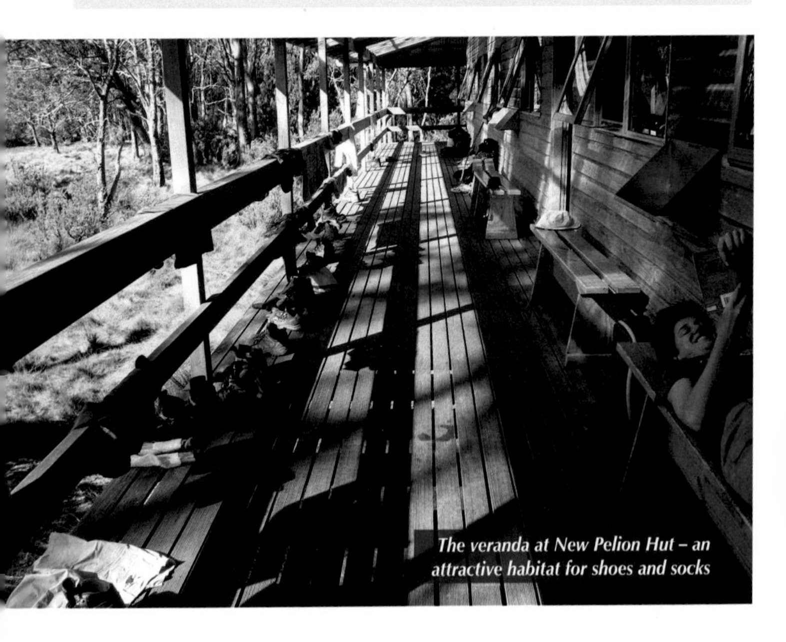

The veranda at New Pelion Hut – an attractive habitat for shoes and socks

Sidetrip: **Mt Oakleigh**

9.2km, 5–6hr return. Total ascent/descent: 625m return. Grade: Medium.

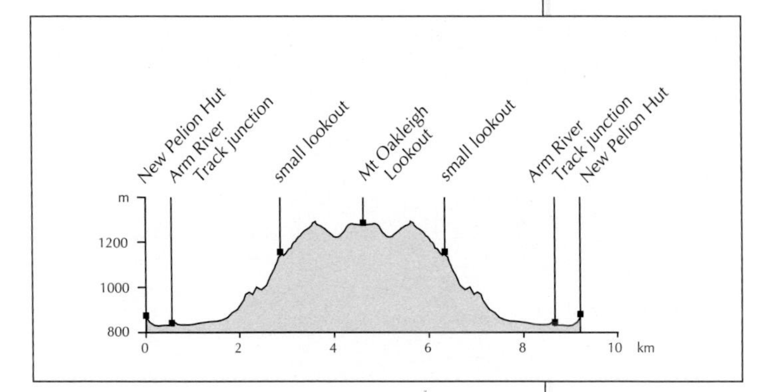

This is one of the best sidetrips on the Overland: not too difficult and with a huge vista as your reward. Duckboards provide a dry route across the sodden plain before the trail enters muddy rainforest. A long, steep climb is made worthwhile by the view from among Mt Oakleigh's huge dolerite spires. The track is sometimes indistinct, both through the rainforest and up on the plateau where it's only marked with cairns, so good visibility is essential. ▸

For a shorter walk, there's a decent lookout about two-thirds of the way up the mountain (5.6km, 2½–3½hr return).

The Mt Oakleigh sidetrip starts from the back of New Pelion Hut. The track heads on to the Pelion Plains over blue-green tussock grass, the path crossed with cider gum roots. The ponds to the right of the track contain Tasmanian froglets, whose sheep-like bleating can often be heard from spring to summer. Cross **Douglas Creek** on a suspension bridge (a good spot for a dip in warmer weather) to arrive at a signposted junction between the Arm River Track and the track for Mt Oakleigh, 560m from New Pelion Hut.

Follow the meandering duckboards across the marshy plain, old moss-covered markers showing the route. ▸

Lizards often laze on the duckboards during sunny weather – watch your step!

Cross a fast-flowing stream on a bridge, beginning to climb slightly as the track enters eucalypts again.

The track passes through a fringe of woolly tea-tree into myrtle beech rainforest, occasional rusted cans on poles and orange triangles indicating the sometimes muddy and indistinct path. Pass an enormous King Billy pine with its deeply fibrous bark – specimens this size have been estimated to be 1000 years old. The myrtles become larger and more dominant further into the rainforest, the track rising in a series of short, sharp bursts separated by interludes of level walking, still with lots of deep, black mud to cross. ◂

The fertile soil means the myrtles are huge, their canopy closed, only moss and glades of mother shieldfern thriving in the gloom.

Finally the climb starts in earnest, the myrtle giving way to a more diverse species mix, including a forest of pandani, which crowd the path, their fronds rustling as you brush past. The vegetation tends lower as it becomes rockier and more exposed, the track continuing to climb steeply. About two-thirds of the way up, 2.8km from New Pelion, a small **lookout** provides a good view over Lake Ayr, Pelion Plains and the surrounding ring of mountains. If you're pressed for time this is a fair compromise for reaching the top.

The vegetation now tends to wiry alpine shrubs as the path winds about, heading generally west. The bulk of the climb is now over and the track, which becomes a little stream after rain, rises gradually with a few rocky scrambles towards the first peak, the occasional small cairn providing guidance.

On top of Mt Oakleigh's plateau, numerous tracks lead towards the mountain's edge. Resist the temptation to follow them too soon, as this first peak's views are incomparable with those further west. ◂

This plateau area is unusual in that it supports five species of skinks – ocellated, metallic and southern grass skinks, as well as northern and southern snow skinks – that aren't usually found together.

Heading west, cross some boulders to follow a deeply eroded track leading into a small gully. From the stream at the bottom of the gully the main **lookout** is 580m away. Climb out of the gully and across weathered boulders to a rocky outcrop near the cliff edge marked with a prominent cairn. This is the best vantage point to look down upon the huge dolerite spires that give Mt Oakleigh its distinctive character, spires formed by the rapid cooling of molten dolerite magma – a formation that doesn't occur on mainland Australia.

On a good day the view is one of the best on the track. At 1280m it's not the highest viewpoint, but perhaps the most interesting, with the terrain of the Overland laid out like a map. There's the serrated edge of Cradle Mountain to the north-west, the bald hill of Mt Emmett near it, and the plateau containing Windermere Hut dotted with lakes. To the south-west there's Mt Pelion West and, moving southwards, other mountains: Mt Achilles (not looking particularly impressive from this angle), the blunt plateau of Mt Thetis, the massive flank of Mt Ossa beside the seemingly low mound of Mt Doris, and then, south-east, the compact double nub of Mt Pelion East (the Overland passes between Mt Pelion East and Mt Doris over the Pelion Gap). ▶

The summit of **Mt Oakleigh** (1286m), whose views are no better than the lookout's, is another 500m to the north.

Retrace your steps and return to New Pelion Hut.

The distinctive profile of Mt Oakleigh

This view, with all the peaks and mountains ranges fading into the blue distance, really make you feel on top of the world.

STAGE 4

New Pelion Hut to Kia Ora Hut

Start	New Pelion Hut
Finish	Kia Ora Hut
Distance	8.6km
Total ascent	335m
Total descent	335m
Grade	Medium
Time	3½–4hr
Maximum altitude	1126m
Possible sidetrips	Mt Ossa (medium–hard); Mt Pelion East (medium)

Initially the track rises gently through diverse forest, getting steeper as it climbs through rainforest to Pelion Gap (1126m) between Mt Pelion East and Mt Doris. From Pelion Gap there's the option to take the sidetrip up Mt Ossa, Tasmania's highest peak (1617m), or a shorter sidetrip to the summit of Mt Pelion East (1466m). From the gap it's an easy descent through gums and moorland to Kia Ora Hut.

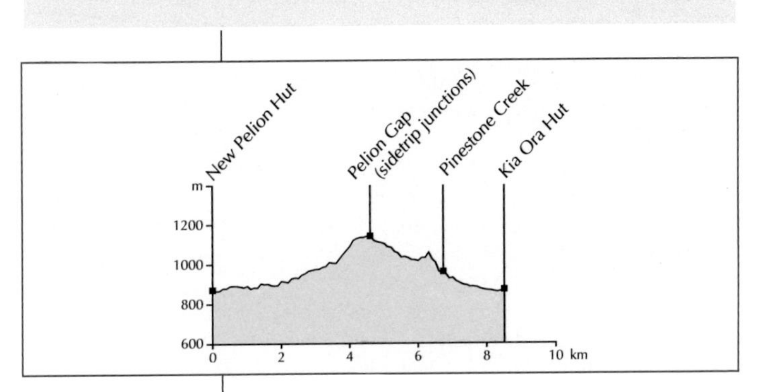

New Pelion Hut to Pelion Gap, 4.5km, 2hr

From New Pelion Hut the track heads south towards Pelion Gap, the pass between the bald head of Mt Doris and the compact chunk of Mt Pelion East. The track gradually climbs, following the **Douglas Creek** valley through mixed forest, boardwalk, duckboards, steps and muddy, rooty sections alternating. The track levels off through cider gum woodland before rising as it enters myrtle rainforest, crossing a stream on a bridge and approaching the Douglas Creek.

About 1.7km from New Pelion, reach a track junction where duckboards wind down 50m to a **waterfall** cascading gracefully down a sloping rock platform in the Douglas.

Back on the Overland, the track climbs slightly, still beside the creek, and enters pencil pine forest, crossing **Snarers Hut Creek** on a substantial bridge, then continuing towards Mt Doris, which peeps through the woodland ahead, Mt Ossa becoming visible to its right.

The track continues its slow climb, winding through a mix of wet and dry forest, levelling off through the deep shade of myrtle rainforest. ▶

A substantial bridge over a fast-flowing tributary of the Douglas offers a good place for a break and a chance to top up on water if you intend to climb Mt Ossa.

A series of split-log boardwalks continues the climb until the track drops into tall myrtle rainforest with a huge hybrid conifer beside the path: a rare cross between a King Billy pine and a pencil pine, *Athrotaxis x laxifolia*. **Pelion Gap** is 950m from here.

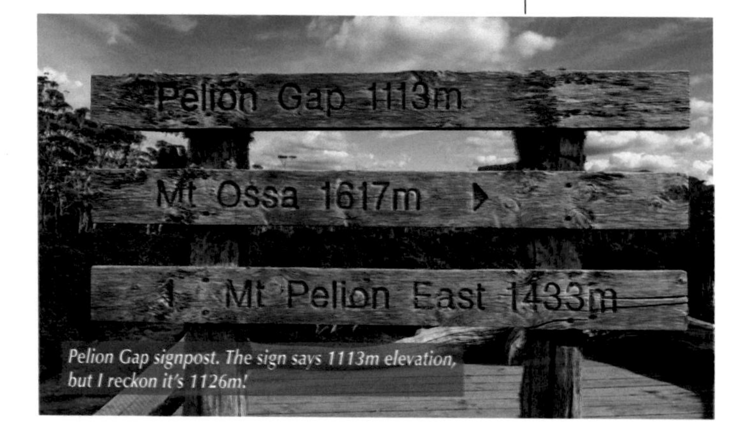

Pelion Gap signpost. The sign says 1113m elevation, but I reckon it's 1126m!

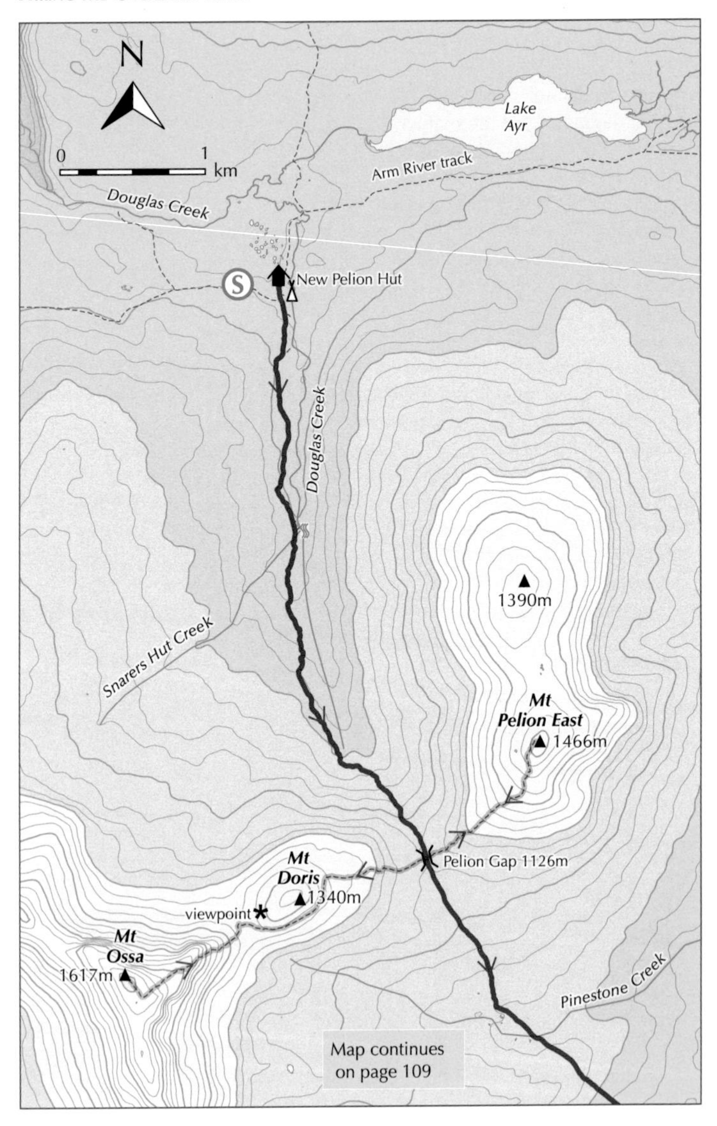
N
0
1
km
Lake
Ayr
Arm River track
Douglas Creek
New Pelion Hut
Douglas Creek
1390m
Snarers Hut Creek
Mt
Pelion East
1466m
Pelion Gap 1126m
Mt
Doris
1340m
viewpoint
Mt
Ossa
1617m
Pinestone Creek
Map continues
on page 109

The real climb soon begins, with stairs rising steeply. As you approach the gap the vegetation becomes more open and alpine, with the path soon arriving at the wide wooden platforms and log seats of the gap. From here there are sidetrips up Mt Ossa and Mt Pelion East.

Sidetrip: Mt Ossa

5.8km, 3½–4½hr return. Total ascent/descent: 605m return. Grade: Medium–hard.

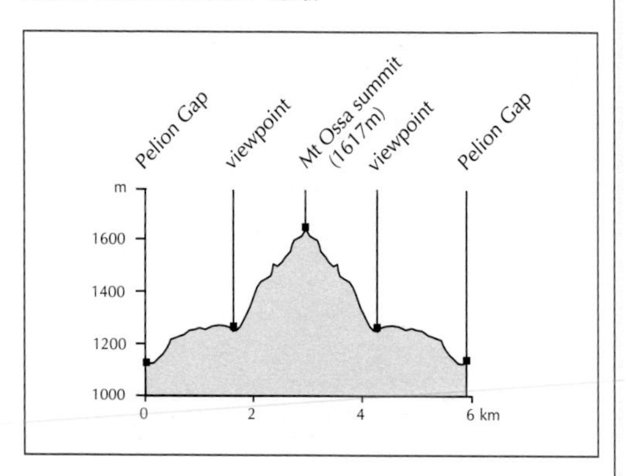

This is one of the most popular sidetrips on the walk, not because the route is easier or the view is better than other mountain sidetrips, but because people like to say they've climbed Tasmania's highest mountain (1617m). Despite its popularity there are a few tricky scrambles which require free hands and a head for heights. ▶ Otherwise, it's a long, steep climb to the first peak of Mt Ossa, after which there's a second, easier, climb to the top. The summit is covered with beautiful smooth boulders offering views in all directions.

For a shorter sidetrip, you can take the Mt Ossa track as far as the lovely alpine meadows of Mt Doris (1340m) and the viewpoint on the saddle between Mt Doris and Mt Ossa (3.2km, 1½–2hr return).

From Pelion Gap head west along the track, soon beginning to climb steeply through scoparia around the south side of Mt Doris. The plants dramatically decrease in size as stairs ascend to a ridge, the views already stunning, the crumbling turrets of Mt Ossa ahead. Follow the ridge over black mesh boardwalk, reaching stairs that resume the climb to the alpine meadows on the upper slopes of **Mt Doris**.

The track levels off on lovely stone paving as it passes to the south of the summit of Mt Doris, a beautiful area of alpine vegetation known as the Japanese Gardens. The challenge of the climb ahead becomes apparent as the seemingly vertical route up the first peak comes into view. About 1.6km from Pelion Gap reach a **viewpoint** at the saddle between Mt Doris and Mt Ossa with good views to the north. This is a decent alternative to the tough climb to the summit.

From the gully the track climbs steeply over boulders and shifting scree, the occasional marker post important to determine the route. Flights of rock steps lead higher with swathes of the lily-like silky milligania nestling among the boulders.

Cross sharply faceted boulders, cleaved from the soaring rock parapets above, with views over the oval Lake McFarlane far below. Traverse a huge rock slab to tackle the last of the climb to the first peak across a wild jumble of stones and boulders. Towards the top the track zigzags right then left, the sheer rock faces all around imposing.

A mountain tarn near the summit of Mt Ossa

A final few tricky scrambles get you to the top of the first peak, the hardest part of the climb now behind you.

The track drops to cross a small gully then climbs steeply again to finally reach the plateau near the summit.

Follow the track over the rock plateau, initially west and then north-west, the occasional marker post indicating the route, to reach the summit where a crown of boulders offers 360° views. The ragged tooth of Cradle Mountain is visible in full, as are all the other peaks along the track, including the impressive Cathedral Mountain towards Kia Ora Hut to the east, the slopes below its fissured bluff littered with rockfalls. Lake St Clair can be spied to the south-east.

Retrace your route and return to Pelion Pass.

Sidetrip: **Mt Pelion East**

2.8km, 1½–2½hr return. Total ascent/descent: 340m return. Grade: Medium.

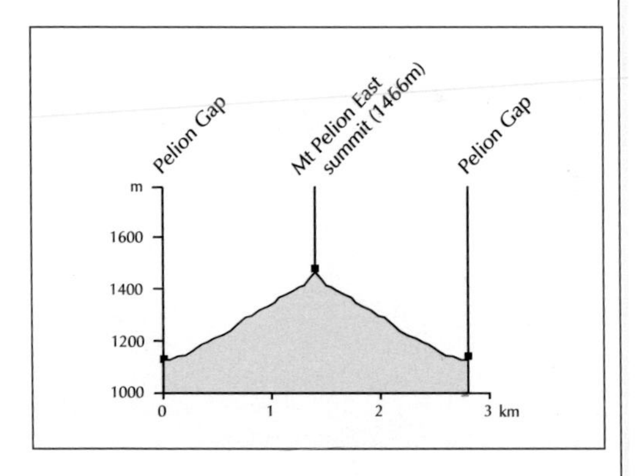

Often overlooked in favour of its more famous neighbour, Mt Ossa, Mt Pelion East (1466m) is a shorter, easier alternative that still rewards with great views. It's a good option when the higher Mt Ossa is in cloud. Although the track is initially muddy and occasionally indistinct, the climb to the compact turret of the summit is surprisingly moderate. A final short, steep scramble, with a few tricky sections requiring free hands, takes you to the top of the dolerite rock stack for a 360° panorama.

This section is particularly glorious in early summer when the scoparia flowers in multicoloured profusion.

From Pelion Gap head north-east, the track initially muddy and deeply eroded. The path climbs gradually through rigid candleheath and snow peppermints to a hillside dense with scoparia, which gets progressively more stunted as the slow climb continues. ◂

The compact turret of **Mt Pelion East** comes into view ahead as split-log boardwalk continues the gradual climb. Steps rise to an even lower landscape of cushion-plants and scattered boulders. The steady climb continues, the sheer nub of the summit seemingly close. The track now picks its way up a slope of fractured dolerite rock and boulders, the path sometimes indistinct, the occasional orange marker indicating the route.

The track turns north-west, curling around the mountain's western flank, small cairns showing the path as it slowly rises to meet the massive stone base of the peak. From here there's a final push to the top, the track heading east to climb steeply up the loose scree and rock, with a few tricky scrambles before reaching the huge, faceted boulders of the summit to be rewarded with incredible views in all directions.

Retrace your route and return to Pelion Gap.

Pelion Gap to Kia Ora Hut, 4.1km, 1½–2hr

From Pelion Gap duckboards head south-east making for easy walking as they descend slowly over a scoparia plain into Pinestone Valley. Ahead, the enormous bluff of Cathedral Mountain with its spill of stone marks the boundary between Cradle Mountain–Lake St Clair National Park and the Walls of Jerusalem National Park.

A rocky path continues the slow descent through central lemon boronia and revolute orites. Pass through snow peppermints with their smooth waxy-feeling trunks, onto a plain with fantastic views back to Mt Ossa, Mt Doris and Mt Pelion East.

The track winds through southern cordrush and alpine coralfern, duckboards over the boggiest areas, before reaching **Pinestone Creek** at the bottom of the

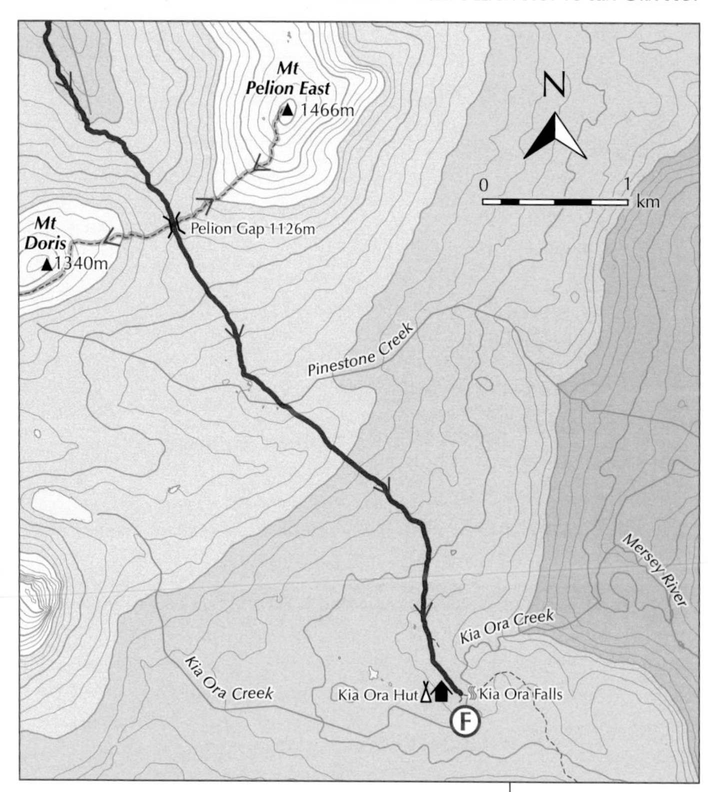

valley, 1.5km from Pelion Gap and 2.6km from Kia Ora Hut.

From the creek the track ascends gently out of the valley through buttongrass and snow peppermints then falls again, initially steeply through woolly tea-tree, before descending more gently through impressive stands of gum-topped stringybark, hedges of wiry bauera lining the path. A narrow unmarked path to the east leads to a private hut; Kia Ora Hut is 460m further on, the sound of **waterfalls** increasing as you approach. Cross a bridge over a small creek to be met by the welcoming sight of the hut.

Kia Ora Hut

KIA ORA HUT

Kia Ora Hut is a small one-room building with a long table and sleeping platforms that can accommodate 20. Set in lovely cider gum woodland, the hut has the spectacular backdrop of the Du Cane Range to the south and the massive escarpment of Cathedral Mountain to the east. Cathedral Mountain is particularly beautiful at sunset. The cool air draining from these surrounding mountains makes the location particularly cold in winter. Kia Ora is approximately the halfway point of the full Overland.

The original hut (since replaced) was built around 1910, one of the circuit of huts Patrick 'Paddy' Hartnett constructed as bases for hunting and snaring. Kia Ora is an informal Maori greeting like 'hi!'. The name is attributed to Paddy Hartnett's brother who visited the area from New Zealand, although it's just as likely to have been coined by Paddy himself, who, aged 12, spent two years in New Zealand working as a bush labourer.

The camping platforms are scattered among the surrounding trees. Seventy metres further along the Overland is Kia Ora Creek, with Kia Ora Falls just downstream of the bridge, accessible by taking the second track to the left after the creek. The lovely little waterfall is a reviving place for a dip.

STAGE 5

Kia Ora Hut to Bert Nichols Hut

Start	Kia Ora Hut
Finish	Bert Nichols Hut
Distance	9.8km
Total ascent	380m
Total descent	350m
Grade	Medium
Time	3½–4½hr
Maximum altitude	1070m
Possible sidetrips	D'Alton and Fergusson Falls (easy–medium); Hartnett Falls (easy)

A fairly short day, leaving plenty of time to enjoy the scenery along the way, including three spectacular waterfalls. The woodlands near Kia Ora Hut change to rainforest as the track approaches the rustic Du Cane Hut. A few kilometres further on there's the opportunity to visit two of the waterfalls, D'Alton and Fergusson Falls, on a short sidetrip. About a kilometre on there's a further sidetrip to Hartnett Falls, perhaps the pick of the three.

A long, steady climb leads to Du Cane Gap (1070m), from where it's a short descent to Bert Nichols Hut.

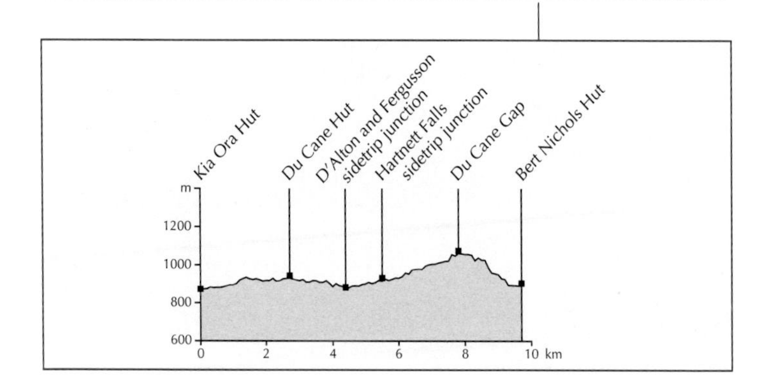

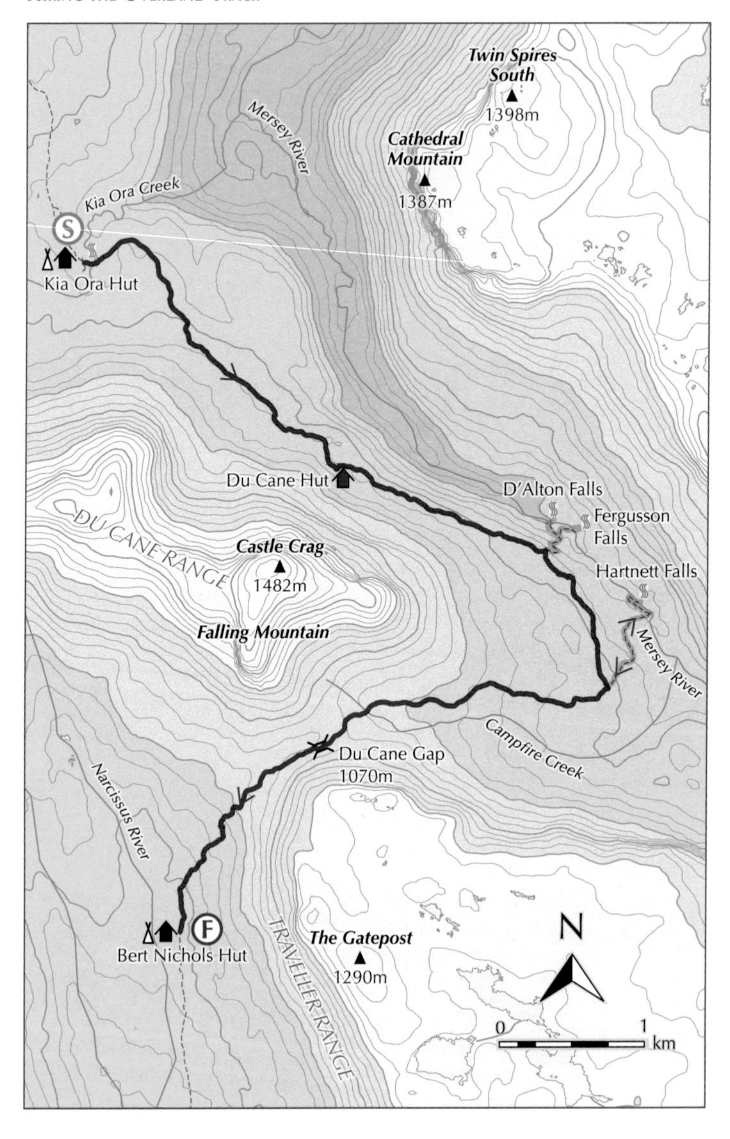
Twin Spires South
1398m
Mersey River
Cathedral Mountain
1387m
Kia Ora Creek
S
Kia Ora Hut
Du Cane Hut
D'Alton Falls
Fergusson Falls
Du Cane Range
Castle Crag
1482m
Hartnett Falls
Falling Mountain
Mersey River
Campfire Creek
Du Cane Gap
1070m
Narcissus River
F
Bert Nichols Hut
The Gatepost
1290m
Traveller Range
N
0
1
km

Kia Ora Hut to Hartnett Falls sidetrip junction, 5.5km, 2hr

Seventy metres east of the Kia Ora Hut cross the **Kia Ora Creek** into a young forest of waxy-trunked snow peppermints. The track gradually rises, the peppermints giving way to gumtopped stringybarks and then a diverse patch of rainforest before entering varied woodland once more. **Castle Crag** (1482m), at the eastern edge of the Du Cane Range, looms to the south-east – the barrier the Overland skirts around on its way to the Du Cane Gap.

Level walking resumes over sections of old boardwalk, crossing a split-log bridge over a tributary to the Mersey River at the edge of the rainforest. All three of today's waterfalls are on the Mersey.

The track twists and undulates over the rainforest's roots and rocks before entering more open leatherwood forest as it approaches **Du Cane Hut**, 2.9km from Kia Ora Hut.

DU CANE HUT

Du Cane Hut is an old shingled cabin in a rainforest clearing. Built in 1910, it's the oldest structure on the Overland. Its well-worn wooden interior, the drunken tilt of its doorways and walls, and its sturdy bush furniture make it the most interesting hut on the track, and the perfect place for a break. (There's also a low-tech outdoor toilet – best in fair weather – up a track just before the hut.)

The hut was built by Paddy Hartnett who worked as a guide, trapper and prospector in the area from around 1908 until 1925. A skilled carpenter, Paddy built the original southern part of the hut out of one huge King Billy pine (the northern part of a hut was added in the 1930s to house the increasing number of bushwalkers). For three winters Paddy's wife and son Billy – one of eight children – also lived here, cooking and helping dry skins by the enormous fireplace, enduring the isolation and primitive conditions. Paddy's work shifted with the seasons: hunting and snaring wallabies and possums in the winter when their fur was at its best, burning off hunting runs in spring, and guiding and prospecting in summer. While he was regarded as a skilled bushman and good guide, the wilderness was a refuge from alcoholism, a problem that grew worse when he moved to other areas to prospect, farm and hunt.

He eventually suffered a stroke in 1938, dying in Hobart in 1944. For his contribution in exploring and introducing the area to others, several features bear his name including the mountain peak Paddy's Nut, Hartnett Rivulet and Hartnett Falls.

Du Cane Hut in the snow

From Du Cane Hut the track descends into deep, dark myrtle beech and sassafras rainforest, occasional split-log boardwalk helping over some muddy sections. The track continues to twist and undulate around the edge of the Du Cane Range, passing a few King Billy pines – their bark conspicuously reddish and fissured.

The plaque to Ranger Fergy

The track becomes even more riven with roots as it descends slightly to reach the **junction** with the sidetrip to D'Alton and Fergusson Falls, 4.3km from Kia Ora Hut. On a myrtle trunk near the sidetrip signpost is a cross-shaped brass plaque in the memory of Ranger Fergy, inscribed 'The Bushwalkers Friend'.

Ranger Albert Dundas Fergusson set up a tourist camp at Cynthia Bay around 1930, later becoming the first ranger in the southern end of the park, constructing many of the original tracks, bridges and huts in the area.

Sidetrip: **D'Alton and Fergusson Falls**

1.7km, 45min return. Total ascent/descent: 120m return. Grade: Easy–medium.

An easy descent through rainforest to a junction where the track branches into two. Both branches end at impressive waterfalls thundering into deep gorges on the Mersey River.

Switchbacks descend through the rainforest on duckboards, split-logs and steps, the descent tapering off to reach a signed junction between the tracks to the two falls.

For **D'Alton Falls** turn left down the slope, crossing a stream then dropping steeply again, the roar of the waterfall, now visible through the trees, growing in volume. As the path approaches the cliff, continue along the side of the ravine, heading away from the falls for 25m. Turn sharply right, an indistinct path leading back towards the falls to view them thundering 25m down into the gorge in a series of cascades. The falls are named after Tom D'Alton, Tasmania's first Minister for Tourists.

For **Fergusson Falls** return to the signed junction and turn right to cross a creek on a split-log bridge. The track remains level, winding over knotted tree roots through lush rainforest. The sound of falling water grows until you emerge by the falls, fierce sheets of water pounding 20m into the river below. ▶

Just below the track is a rock platform where you can sit, the waterfall rushing past just metres away from your face. When Ranger Fergy died in 1970 his ashes were scattered here.

Retrace your steps to return to the main track.

Back on the main track, the Overland continues from the junction through beautiful rainforest containing King Billy pine, sassafras and leatherwood, the occasional gumtopped stringybark soaring high above the canopy. The thickly knotted roots that cover the path make the going a little slow, but after 1.1km arrive at the signposted **junction** with the sidetrip to **Hartnett Falls**.

Sidetrip: **Hartnett Falls**

2.2km, 1–1½hr return. Total ascent/descent: 85m return. Grade: Easy.

From the junction, the track gently descends through relatively open rainforest, massive stringybarks towering

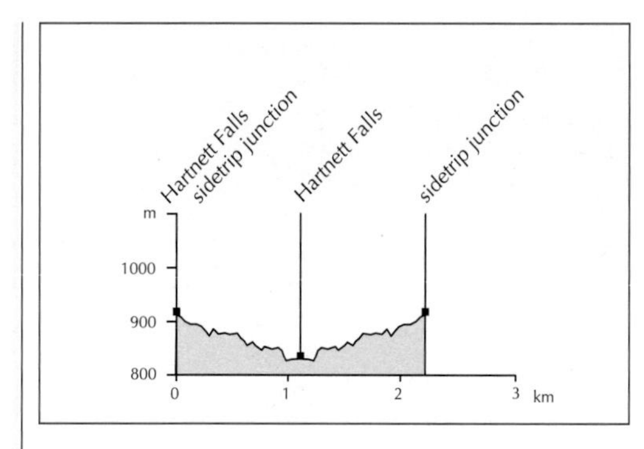

Although there's a swimming hole above the falls, the best spot is 300m the opposite direction, at the base of the falls.

over the myrtle. The occasionally wet path then falls steadily before levelling off through mixed woodland, the sound of the waterfall rising through snow peppermints, alpine heathmyrtle crowding the path. The track continues through a buttongrass field then crosses duckboards to arrive at a clearing beside the top of the **waterfall**, 700m from the main track. ◂

Continue west along the track parallel to the river, heading downstream along a path through the thick scrub. The track descends towards the river, entering mossy rainforest and then turning right to cross a beautiful little tributary of the Mersey. Head upstream along the riverbank towards the base of the falls.

> **Hartnett Falls** are a compact funnel of water roaring 30m down a cliff face, eons of flow having worn a channel in the rock. The more adventurous can wade into the pool at the base of the falls where there's a deep swimming hole among the blasting spray. Even aside from the falls, the Mersey River provides a tranquil place for a break.

Return the way you came to rejoin the Overland Track.

Stage 5 has waterfalls aplenty – D'Alton Falls

Hartnett Falls sidetrip junction to Bert Nichols Hut, 4.3km, 2hr

The main track continues from the junction of the Hartnett Falls sidetrip through mixed rainforest-woodland, the track initially level but still damp, rooty and rocky. The track begins to climb slowly, passing through a pocket of celery-top and King Billy pines, the track drying out as it climbs out of the Mersey Valley towards the Du Cane Gap.

The Overland now climbs steadily, steps and board-walk leading through an interesting mix of rainforest, moorland and woodland species, **Castle Crag** appearing ahead. The track levels off before rising again through snow peppermints until crossing **Campfire Creek** on large stepping stones, 1.8km from the Hartnett Falls junction and 500m from Du Cane Gap.

The path continues to rise, finally reaching **Du Cane Gap** (1070m), marked by a sign on a dead tree. ◂ Bert Nichols Hut is 1.9km away.

To the west, Falling Mountain in the Du Cane Range forms one side of the gap, while the Traveller Range to the south forms the other. The boulders here make a good place for a break.

The track gradually descends through beautifully varied forest including wiry bauera, spreading cheeseberry and mountain needlebush, stepping stones helping cross muddy areas as you enter the Narcissus Valley, the valley that leads all the way to Lake St Clair, and part of the Derwent River catchment.

Enormous, straight, smooth-barked alpine yellow gums mark the descent into myrtle rainforest. The track falls steeply then crosses two bridges over tributaries of the Narcissus River, gumtopped stringybarks rising overhead, before the track leaves the rainforest and levels off, passing several camping platforms before arriving at **Bert Nichols Hut**.

BERT NICHOLS HUT

Completed in 2009 to replace the ageing – and now demolished – Windy Ridge Hut, the $1.2 million Bert Nichols Hut is an enormous structure with a high roof and modern design. The hut is named in honour of Bert Nichols, trapper, guide, ranger and Overland Track pioneer. There's an optimistic clothes 'drying area', three bunk rooms each with two sleeping shelves (accommodating a total of 24) and a cavernous dining room with plenty of tables and skylights. There's even art – yes art! Giant leaf skeletons hanging from the dining room ceiling, part of a government requirement for art in public buildings. All of which makes the little gas heater tacked on a wall seem a little inadequate.

Bert Nichols Hut

As the sleeping-quarters are separated from the dining area they are quiet but cold during winter. During this time some hikers sleep in the dining room near the heater, although it struggles to warm the room.

To the west of the hut the rocky cone of Mt Geryon and the prominence of The Acropolis make for a spectacular backdrop. The Acropolis is the peak you can climb on the sidetrip from Pine Valley Hut, part of the Du Cane Range, which, together with the Traveller Range, form a massive cirque 3km wide and 500m deep, the former head of the huge glacier that stretched all the way down the Narcissus Valley past Cynthia Bay.

There are at least 10 camping platforms among the trees, including a secluded one on the way to the toilets. The group camping platform is built around a grand, spreading myrtle.

STAGE 6

Bert Nichols Hut to Narcissus Hut

Start	Bert Nichols Hut
Finish	Narcissus Hut
Distance	10.1km
Total ascent	165m
Total descent	310m
Grade	Easy
Time	2¾–3¾hr
Maximum altitude	896m
Possible sidetrips	Pine Valley Hut (easy, best overnight), with further sidetrips to The Labyrinth (medium–hard) and The Acropolis (hard)

One of the most beautiful sections on the Overland, the track paralleling the (mostly hidden) Narcissus River all day. The mix of habitats – woodland, wetland, rainforest and moorland – means there's rich birdlife. The walking is made all the more enjoyable by the level, mostly dry path, which follows a lateral moraine, a ridge of material left behind at the edge of a retreating glacier – the same body of ice that created the valley's wide 'U' shape and helped form Lake St Clair.

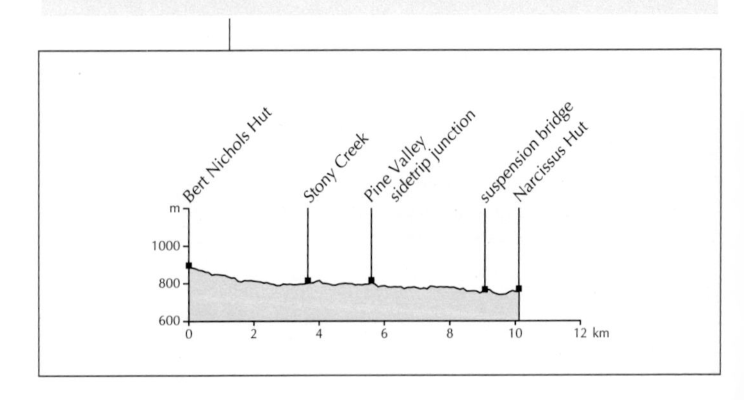

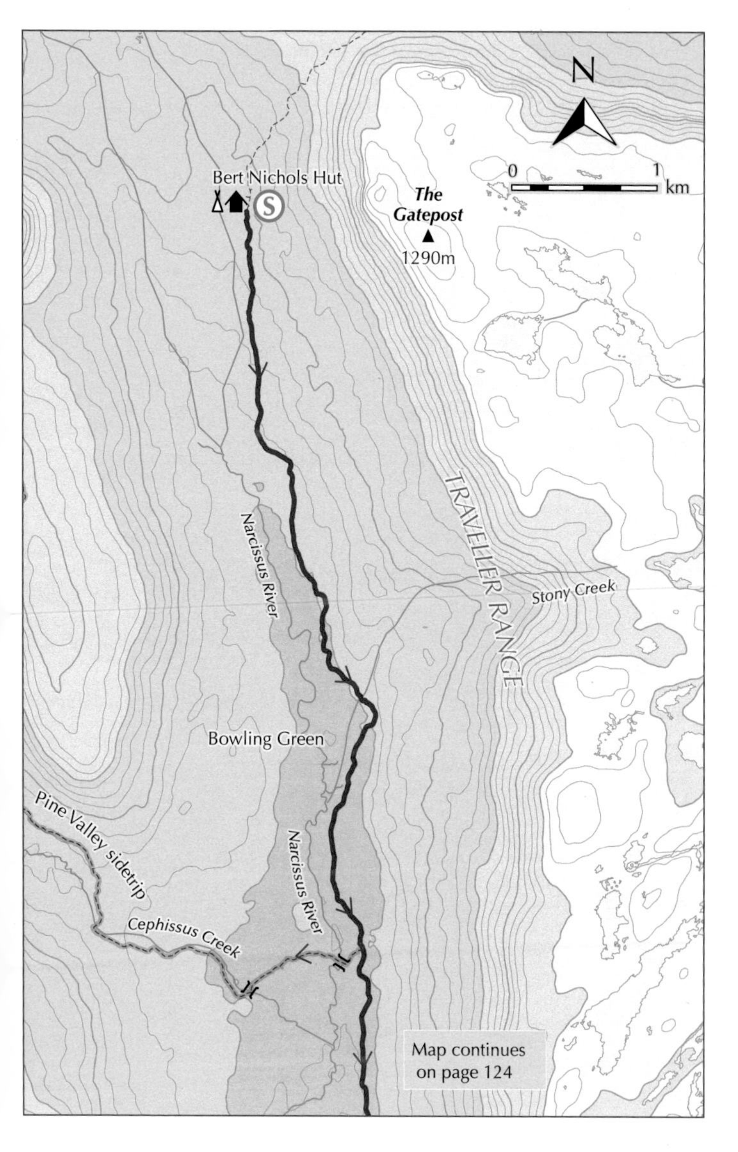
N
0
1
km
Bert Nichols Hut
S
The Gatepost
1290m
TRAVELLER RANGE
Stony Creek
Narcissus River
Bowling Green
Narcissus River
Pine Valley sidetrip
Cephissus Creek
Map continues on page 124

Bert Nichols Hut to Pine Valley sidetrip junction, 5.7km, 1½–2hr

From Bert Nichols Hut the track undulates through woolly tea-tree and gumtopped stringybark into woodland featuring Tasmanian waratahs, mountain needlebush and silver banksia. The track descends gradually, the walking easy, with stepping stones across muddy areas. The forest begins to open up, giant stringybarks rising from the mixed forest, the jigsaw of habitats suiting a variety of birdlife.

After 2.7km, cross a lovely stream on a substantial bridge with a handrail, the stream's banks reinforced with planks. The path soon falls to cross a second stream with a wooden bench. Cabbage gums begin to dominate, the track slowly descending to reach **Stony Creek**, 3.8km from Bert Nichols Hut, a shallow rivulet on the edge of a rainforest pocket, and a peaceful place for a break.

The woodland soon resumes, with the **Bowling Green** to the west, an open field formed from a combination of frost and marsupial grazing and often the location of raucous frog-calls. The track crosses several creeks to arrive at the **junction** of the Pine Valley sidetrip.

Sidetrip: **Pine Valley Hut**

4.9km, 1½–2hr one way. Ascent/descent: 150m/100m one way. Grade: Easy.

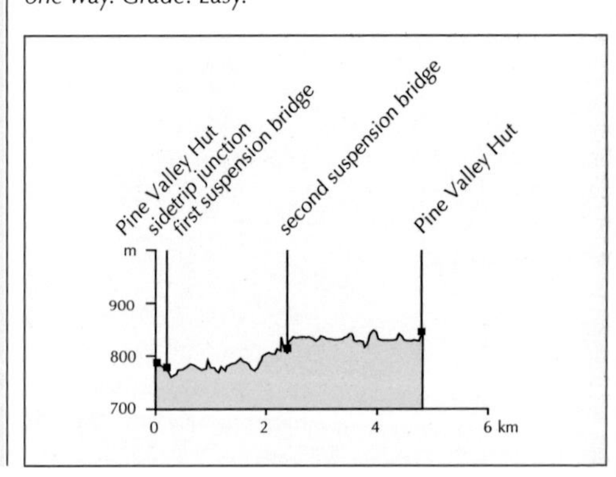

Named Pine Valley after the stands of King Billy, celerytop and pencil pines that line the upper Cephissus Creek, Pine Valley Hut is deep among some of the finest cool temperate rainforest in Australia – one of highlights of the walk for many Overlanders. Being off the main track promotes the feeling of being somewhere secluded and special (although the hut can sometimes be busy during the summer holidays when Tasmanians hike into the valley from Narcissus Hut). This sidetrip is best enjoyed by staying overnight, which allows time to visit The Labyrinth and/or The Acropolis – two of the best sidetrips on the track.

The track to Pine Valley Hut is fairly level and well defined, crossing two suspension bridges as it leads further up the valley, entering rainforest that grows more ancient, mossy and mysterious as you approach the hut.

From the junction, the track meanders through cabbage gums for 180m to a metal **suspension bridge** over the **Narcissus River**. Duckboards then pass through dense hedges of alpine heathmyrtle before climbing slightly over roots and rocks to follow a ridge. Cross a small buttongrass moor on boardwalk and duckboards to a reach a **bridge** across the **Cephissus Creek**, 1km from the turn-off with the main track.

Continue through beautiful woodland beside the creek, boardwalk sections making for easy walking between numerous rocky rises, before arriving at another sweeping suspension bridge, this time back over the Cephissus, 2.4km from Pine Valley Hut.

The track passes through mixed woodland with giant pandani, the surface getting muddy and more root-bound. The forest begins to become more enclosed, the appearance of celerytop pines signalling a plunge into the deep, mossy green world of myrtle rainforest, and with it, as usual, the track becomes muddier.

The path descends a little, still parallelling the creek, the rainforest punctured by the massive trunks of alpine yellow gums, a wetland becoming visible in the valley below. ▶

Bright red bracket fungi can sometimes be found in this area, more luminous in the dim rainforest than even the orange trail-markers.

After crossing a knoll, long stretches of split-log boardwalk span some muddy areas and lead to a mossy

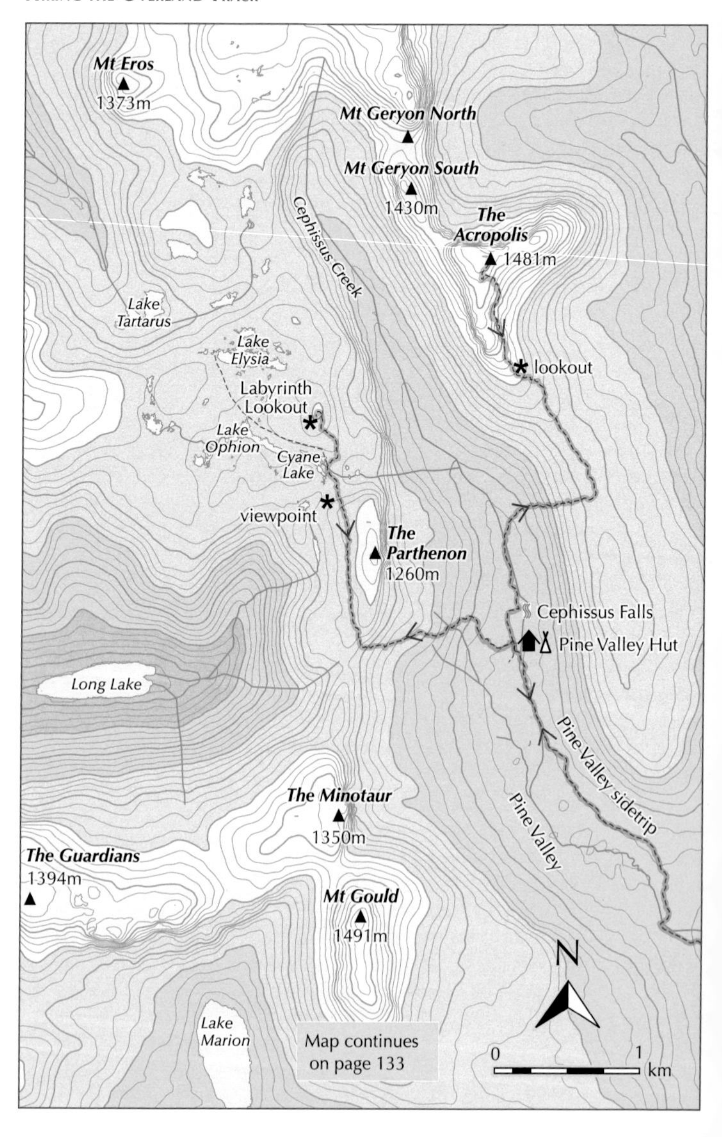
Mt Eros
1373m
Mt Geryon North
Mt Geryon South
1430m
The Acropolis
1481m
Cephissus Creek
Lake Tartarus
Lake Elysia
Labyrinth Lookout
lookout
Lake Ophion
Cyane Lake
viewpoint
The Parthenon
1260m
Cephissus Falls
Pine Valley Hut
Long Lake
Pine Valley sidetrip
Pine Valley
The Minotaur
1350m
The Guardians
1394m
Mt Gould
1491m
N
Lake Marion
0
1
km

Map continues on page 133

rainforest wonderland. About 500m from a hut a long wavy boardwalk crosses the creek and follows its graceful curves. Crossing the creek for the last time, the track enters hushed, otherworldly rainforest, a sign soon announcing your arrival at **Pine Valley Hut**.

PINE VALLEY HUT

Pine Valley Hut is a simple, dim single-roomed hut similar to Kia Ora, with a long bench and four sleeping shelves accommodating 24. There's a coal-fed pot-bellied stove for heating. The original hut was built by Ranger Fergy in the early 1940s but has been rebuilt and renovated several times since then.

The camping at Pine Valley Hut is limited. There are four camping platforms as well as several level campsites along the creek.

FURTHER SIDETRIPS FROM PINE VALLEY HUT

The Labyrinth Lookout: 7.2km, 4–5hr return. Total ascent/descent: 560m return. Grade: Medium–hard.

The Acropolis: 8.2km, 5–6hr return. Total ascent/descent: 840m return. Grade: Hard.

The warnings about The Labyrinth and The Acropolis on the signboards at Pine Valley Hut are enough to make you want to bolt the hut's door and hide under the table. While the warnings might seem overdone, several hikers have died in this area, so the advice on the boards needs to be heeded. Both sidetrips should only be done in reasonably good weather, with warm clothing, water, GPS, map, compass, first aid kit, wet weather gear and spare food – and never alone.

Sidetrip: The Labyrinth Lookout

7.2km, 4–5hr return. Total ascent/descent: 560m return. Grade: Medium–hard.

The name's a little misleading: while the geography of The Labyrinth is complicated, it isn't so much an enclosed maze as an open plateau, an alternate world of huge, weathered, lichen-spotted boulders, rounded hills, lakes and alpine vegetation. It's an area that would look at home in Scandinavia, which makes it all the more

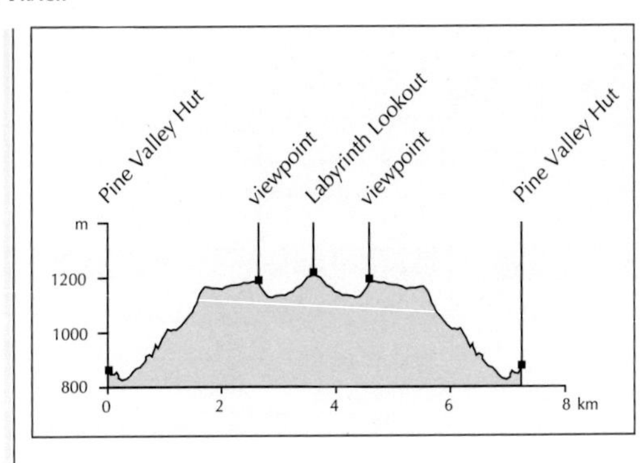

The name Labyrinth is correct in one sense: it's easy to become disoriented in this landscape – groups need to be well prepared in order to explore this area in safety.

remarkable to discover it here. ◂ As all the lakes indicate, the paths in this area can be very wet. In summer there can be an abundance of ants which can be a nuisance. The tracks on the plateau are only marked with small, irregular cairns. The climb to The Labyrinth plateau is very steep in parts, but at least it's short and sharp. An option for a shorter walk (5.2km, 1½–2hr return) is the viewpoint over Cyane Lake.

This is gorgeous rainforest, the track drifting through a world of soft moss and twisted tree roots.

The narrow track starts behind the hut and winds 60m through myrtle beech, giant pandani and King Billy pine to the junction with the sidetrip to The Acropolis. Taking a left, pass an enormous gumtopped stringybark as the track begins to climb slowly, the orange trail-markers defining the sometimes indistinct path. ◂ The path starts to rise more steeply through huge, ancient King Billy pines and myrtle beech, their gnarled roots and rocks providing steps. About 800m from the start of the track the climb becomes even steeper as it ascends a rocky streambed before entering stunted rainforest, the rate of ascent slowing through deeply tangled roots and rocks.

The vegetation becomes even more stunted as the track continues to climb, then levels off through a mix of rainforest, woodland and alpine species as it rounds the rocky spire of **The Parthenon** (1260m), with views back along the Pine and Narcissus valleys to Lake St Clair. The track now begins a very steep haul to the plateau, step-like rocks assisting on the tough climb.

Cyane Lake from the viewpoint

Reaching the gap (1165m, 1.7km from the hut, 1hr) to the east of The Parthenon, a level section parallels its rocky ridge north through stunted, twisted snow peppermints and over smooth stone slabs, occasional cairns indicating the track. The path gradually rises to reach the plateau until, 2.6km from the hut, the **viewpoint** over **Cyane Lake** is reached. From here there's a view into The Labyrinth's spectacular netherworld of tarns, lakes, huge rock slabs and scattered pencil pines, with the bluff of **The Acropolis** framing the scene to the north-east.

If time and weather permit, descend steeply over rock slabs and boulders towards Cyane Lake, occasional cairns marking the route. After 200m reach an indistinct junction and take the right turn, the track climbing slowly to the north-west. Continue following the small cairns for 240m through pencil pine and beautiful lichen-spotted boulders towards the north-east tip of Cyane Lake to reach a signed junction. The track to the left leads to Lake Elysia (1.1km to the north-west), while the track to the right leads to The Labyrinth Lookout (550m to the north).

On a clear day the view is spectacular; north-east to The Acropolis, south-east past The Parthenon down to Lake St Clair, and to the north-west across the wonderland of The Labyrinth to Lake Elysia and beyond.

Compared to the climb to the plateau, the 80m climb to The **Labyrinth Lookout** (1213m) is easy. From the junction, follow the track through dwarf pines and bonsaied deciduous beech, cairns still occasionally indicating the route. The path rises in stages, passing behind a smaller peak and flattening off before climbing more steeply through twisted, wizened pencil pines towards the summit of the smooth, nameless peak – part of the Du Cane Range. The summit is marked by a waist-high cairn. ◂

Retrace your steps and return to Pine Valley Hut.

Sidetrip: The Acropolis

8.2km, 5–6hr return. Total ascent/descent: 840m return. Grade: Hard.

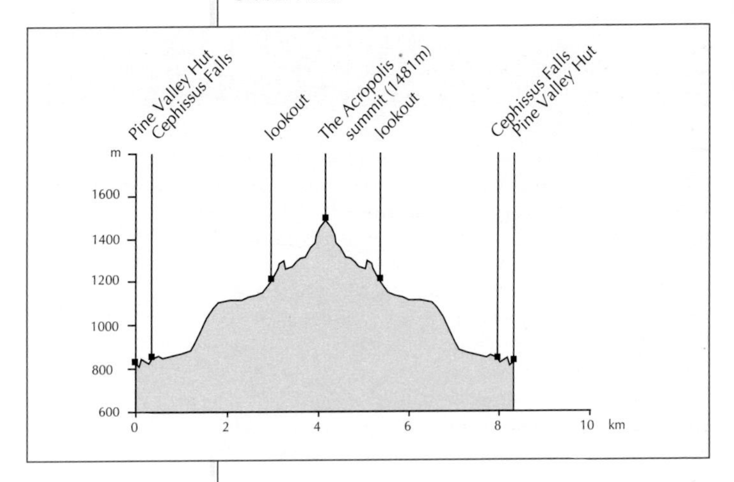

There is no reliable water source after Cephissus Falls – bring enough for the day.

For fairly fit folk this is one of the best sidetrips on the Overland, a reasonably well-marked, relatively dry track through some of the most ancient and spectacular cool temperate rainforest in Australia. On the way you'll encounter Cephissus Falls, huge trees and a steep climb to the beautiful park-like alpine vegetation of the plateau. ◂ Then it's a cruise through snow peppermints to another steep climb, this one over fractured dolerite rocks and boulders with one particularly tricky section needing free hands and a stout heart. The view from the top (1481m) is incredible, looking down on the stone pinnacles that might have given the mountain its name. A shorter alternative is a lookout on the peak's lower slope that offers great views over the mountains to the south (5.8km return, 3–4 hr).

Like The Labyrinth sidetrip, this sidetrip also starts from the junction 60m behind the hut. From the turn-off the path undulates through awe-inspiring rainforest with groves of tall, thin shaggy-bearded pandani, huge King Billy pines and massive alpine yellow gums. After 350m arrive at **Cephissus Falls**, just off the main track, several tiers of lovely cascades flowing into a wide pool.

The track continues away from the creek, still fairly level as it ducks among pandani, sporadic orange trackmarkers and old, red-painted blazes showing the narrow winding trail. Cross **Cephissus Creek** on a log then continue over boggy ground on split-log boardwalk and bridges, the moss becoming even thicker and all enveloping.

A kilometre from the hut the track skirts around what would have to be a contender for the biggest myrtle beech on the Overland, although there are several other contenders nearby. ▶

Mature myrtles can be thirty metres high and between 400 and 600 years-old.

The track begins to climb steeply through the rainforest; a long climb with little respite. The rate of ascent finally slackens as the track winds through small pandani and enters a twisted grove of deciduous beech looking like an orchard gone wild. After about an hour emerge onto the plateau 1.8km from the hut and 1100m in elevation. Nearly half of the climb is now over and there's the chance to catch your breath before the next ascent as you cross the plateau.

Duckboards lead across the plateau's alpine vegetation with alpine heathmyrtle, pencil pines and snow peppermints scattered in a park-like setting. **The Acropolis** rises to the north-east with its amazing spine of free-standing dolerite columns visible near its summit.

Crossing the plateau towards The Acropolis (photo: Yasmin Kelsall)

The path continues north-east, heading directly towards the mountain, the duckboards ending 600m from the lookout and 1.8km from the summit, as the track begins a long, slow climb through lovely snow peppermint woodland towards the base of The Acropolis. The track gets progressively steeper and rockier, rising rapidly to a rocky outcrop a few hundred metres from the mountain's sheer base which provides a superb **lookout** with views over Narcissus Valley to Lake St Clair and the flat top of Mt Olympus. From here the summit is about 1.2km away. This is a good alternative to the summit if pressed for time or if the conditions aren't suitable to tackle the difficult climb to the top.

The track resumes its steep climb, the rocks getting larger and the vegetation falling away. The path levels off as it winds its way beneath the sheer flank of the mountain towards a boulder field. Free hands become essential to clamber over the jumbled spill of rocks, dense banks of silky milligania adding some green to the scene, occasional orange marker-posts still indicating the route. The path levels off again, still slowly skirting The Acropolis's eastern side, heading for the dolerite pinnacles near the summit. The final, very steep section requires picking through boulders and rocks towards a chute to the left of the pinnacles. This section in particular requires some athleticism, two free hands and a bit of nerve, particularly one – and just one – tricky scramble over a chest high cube of rock. After this challenge it's relatively easy going until suddenly, triumphantly, the top is reached, or at least a peak just below the summit. Note the cairn here beside the chute: you'll need to locate it again on your return from the summit, 150m north-east across a crazy jumble of boulders.

On a clear day **the view** from the top is superb, overlooking the huge dolerite pinnacles that stand like totems between The Acropolis and the conical peak of Mt Geryon – itself an amazing summit, composed of fractured columns felled by the relentless freeze and thaw of water. To the east, Bert Nichols Hut can be seen nestled in the Narcissus Valley, the valley which the Overland follows all the way to Lake St Clair to the south-east. To the west is the wavy 'Y' shape of Lake Elysia in the otherworldly expanse of The Labyrinth.

Retrace your steps and return to Pine Valley Hut.

Pine Valley sidetrip junction to Narcissus Hut, 4.4km, 1¼–1¾hr

From the junction the easy walking continues, the track rolling and winding but still generally heading south down the Narcissus Valley towards Lake St Clair. ▶ Cross a creek on a boardwalk which continues into a field of alpine coralfern, the flat top of Mt Olympus coming into view far down the valley beside the still-hidden Lake St Clair. The boardwalk snakes for 200m before entering tall, straight gumtopped stringybark forest. The track becomes rocky, the vegetation still the most varied of the Overland, passing an **enormous stringybark** 2.3km from the Pine Valley turnoff, whose massive roots make a fine place for a break.

Giant cabbage gums dominate the beautiful mixed woodland, patches of woolly tea-tree indicating damper areas.

The path passes through a small pocket of rainforest, seemingly still and quiet after the woodland, with a sinuous boardwalk continuing on the other side along the rainforest fringe. Another long boardwalk leads into spectacular buttongrass moorland, Mt Olympus drawing closer, the conical Mt Byron to its right. The boardwalk leads all the way to an impressive steel **suspension bridge** over the Narcissus River, 1.2km from Narcissus Hut.

The track continues through cabbage gum woodland with a dense understorey of western sheoak, silver banksia and mountain needlebush. After crossing a swampy area the track enters open forest beside the river, a scene that compels a break even if one's not required. Soon after the two little **brown huts of Narcissus** come into view beneath the impressive boughs of the cabbage gums near the river. The first hut is for rangers, the second for hikers.

The suspension bridge over the Narcissus River

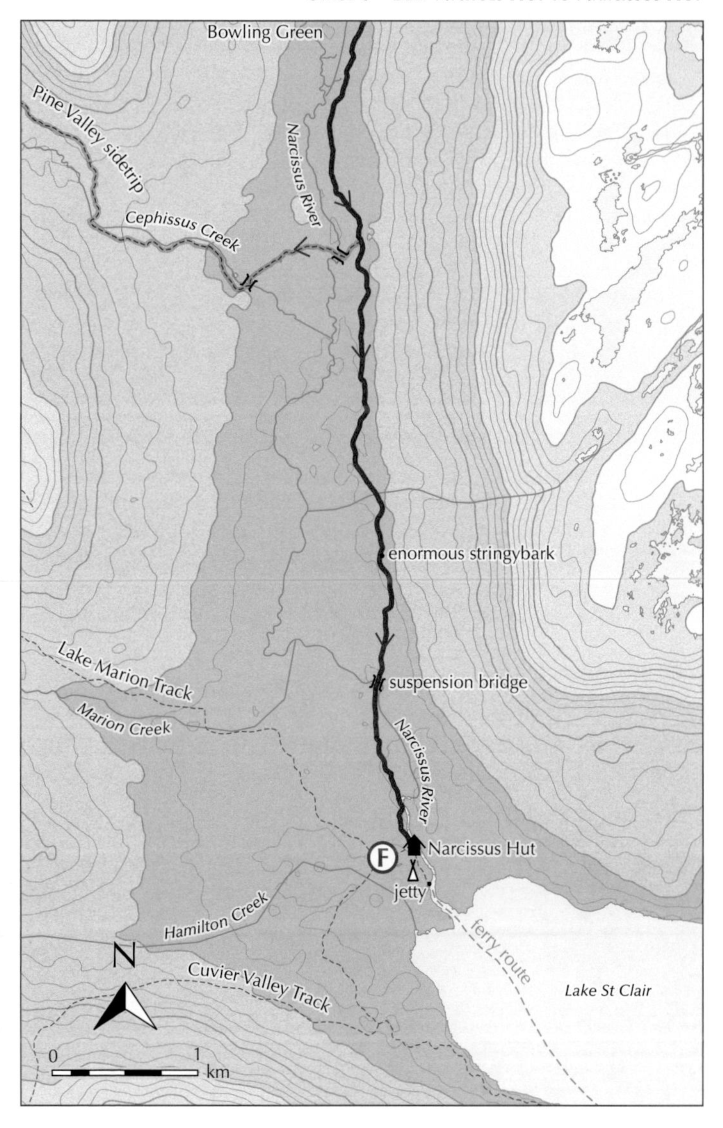
Bowling Green
Pine Valley sidetrip
Narcissus River
Cephissus Creek
enormous stringybark
Lake Marion Track
suspension bridge
Marion Creek
Narcissus River
F
Narcissus Hut
jetty
Hamilton Creek
ferry route
N
Cuvier Valley Track
Lake St Clair
0
1
km

NARCISSUS HUT

Narcissus Hut can sleep 18 on two sleeping shelves, with a separate dining room containing a table, benches and gas heater. The hut can erupt with mice after dark: make sure you hang your food out of reach.

There are four camping platforms and a table behind the hut or, 100m along the track towards the jetty, a small boardwalk to the left leads to a flat, sandy camping area beside the river. Toilets are along the path behind the hut, near where the Overland continues towards Echo Point.

In the evening, just before dusk, platypuses can sometimes be spotted from the jetty, 300m from the hut, near where the Narcissus River enters Lake St Clair. The jetty also makes a good place for a dip.

Although many hikers hurry through here in their haste to catch the ferry, Narcissus Hut has plenty of character and makes a good base from which to explore the Lake St Clair area.

Lake St Clair, at 167m deep, is Australia's deepest natural lake, the result of three glaciers converging to gouge out the trough; one along the Narcissus Valley, one along Pine Valley and the third from Lake Marion. On a calm day you can understand why the Aboriginals knew the lake as *Leeawuleena*, 'Sleeping Water'.

Narcissus Jetty, the place to look for a platypus at dusk

FERRY

Many hikers choose to take the 20–30 minute ferry ride across Lake St Clair rather than hiking 17.2km around the lake through rainforest. The Lake St Clair ferry, the *Ida Clair*, leaves from the jetty 300m south of the hut. The ferry can carry a maximum of 22 passengers, although in rough weather it may be unable to operate.

The radio in the hut is for contacting the ferry – from 8:30am to 6pm – to make or confirm bookings, or else you can call them on 03 6289 1137. If you've booked a ferry, but have taken a day or two longer to reach the hut, no problem – there's no cancellation fee, you'll just have to use the radio to make a new booking. The ferry might not run if there are no bookings. As with all schedules, the one below is subject to change: please confirm prices and times. Taking the ferry across Lake St Clair cuts a day from hiking the Overland.

During peak season the ferry schedule is:

- Depart Cynthia Bay: 9:00am, 12:30pm, 3:00pm
- Depart Narcissus Hut: 9:45am, 1:15pm, 3:45pm
- Arrive Cynthia Bay: 10:30am, 2:00pm, 4:30pm

In winter the ferry only operates if there are bookings. If less than six people are on the ferry, a minimum of charge of $300 applies. If six or more people want an additional ferry (or fewer people are willing to pay the price of six) they will often put on an extra service.

The ferry costs an eye-watering $50 for adults, $25 for children 5–12 years and is free for under 5s. If taking the ferry north towards Narcissus Hut you can arrange to be dropped at Echo Point Hut for $42. Pick-ups from Echo Point are only possible if arranged and paid for beforehand.

STAGE 7

Narcissus Hut to Cynthia Bay

Start	Narcissus Hut
Finish	Cynthia Bay
Distance	17.2km
Total ascent	710m
Total descent	710m
Grade	Easy–medium
Time	5–7hr
Maximum altitude	780m

Many hikers miss the final day of the Overland, opting to catch the ferry across Lake St Clair to Cynthia Bay. But for those not suffering rainforest fatigue there's plenty to enjoy on this section, including lovely open woodland at the start and end of the walk and a dense canopy of myrtle beech in between. Echo Point Hut, with its own little beach and jetty, is the most charming sleeping hut on the track and a great place for a break. Although there are a few rooty, muddy sections in the rainforest, it's generally a level, easy walk around the edge of the lake with the chance to observe the shifting balance between rainforest and woodland.

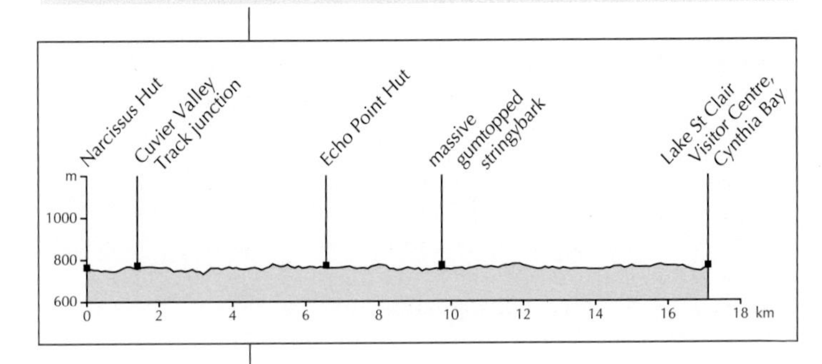

Narcissus Hut to Echo Point Hut, 6.5km, 2–3hr

The Overland resumes behind Narcissus Hut, arriving after 220m at a junction with the **Lake Marion Track** (if you wish to visit Lake Marion, allow 4½–5½hr for the 11km return trip). Remaining on the Overland Track, a raised boardwalk soon continues through woolly tea-tree across a swampy area known as Hamilton Crossing. Lake St Clair is close, but still hidden from view.

Crossing a damp, grassy field reveals the flat top of **Mt Olympus** ahead, under whose heights most of the day will be spent. The walking is easy as the winding track becomes soft with leaf litter as it enters a forest of enormous eucalypts, with mountain peppers and Tasmanian waratahs also becoming abundant. The rainforest soon begins to appear, myrtle beech and celerytop pines becoming more common until the green-tinged world of the rainforest is entered once more.

After 1.6km reach the **junction** with the alternative route to Cynthia Bay via the Cuvier Valley (the valley behind Mt Olympus) signed 'Byron Gap', a muddier, poorly marked path which takes an additional 2–3hr. Continue straight, towards Echo Point Hut, the track becoming muddy and rooty in parts. At the site of an enormous gumtopped stringybark – at least 10m around the base – cross a creek into ancient myrtle beech forest, the myrtle's trunks covered with a miniature world of mosses and lichens.

Glimpses of the lake begin to appear through the trees, until 3.2km from Narcissus Hut there's finally a chance to duck out to a gravel beach beside the lake with great views back towards Narcissus Valley, Mt Gould and the rugged spires of The Acropolis. ▶

Looking north-east, across the lake, the sharp fin of Mt Ida rises from the Traveller Range.

Lake St Clair was flooded for a hydroelectric scheme in 1937, raising the water level by 3m, covering most of the beautiful beaches early visitors commented upon, and leading to the tangles of dead trees that often line the shore today.

The track continues to skirt the lake's edge, this fairly long, undulating and often muddy section crossing a series of small streams, the track rising away from the lake, then returning periodically. About 1.8km from Echo

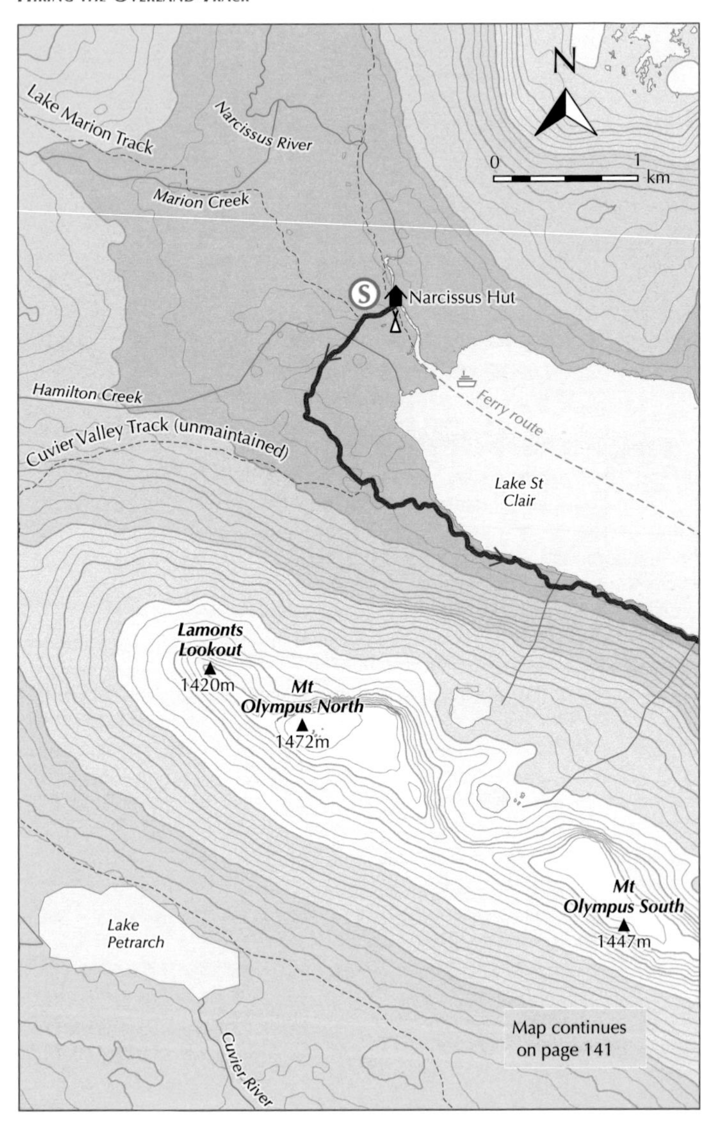
N
0
1
km
Lake Marion Track
Narcissus River
Marion Creek
Narcissus Hut
Hamilton Creek
Cuvier Valley Track (unmaintained)
Ferry route
Lake St Clair
Lamonts Lookout
1420m
Mt Olympus North
1472m
Mt Olympus South
1447m
Lake Petrarch
Cuvier River
Map continues on page 141

Lake St Clair from the rainforest

Point Hut cross a series of three plastic mesh bridges over small creeks near the lake.

Finally a series of boardwalks lead to a bridge over a fast-flowing stream that has cut a deep channel through the soft rainforest floor. From here **Echo Point Hut** is 200m.

ECHO POINT HUT

Echo Point Hut is a battered wooden cabin beneath the rainforest canopy at the edge of the lake, with its own jetty, a small crescent of beach and views across to the cone of Mt Ida.

Water comes from the lake or the creek beside the cabin. The cabin is small, sleeping only eight, and has a coal heater. The toilet is just across the creek towards Cynthia Bay and up the hill. The log book is kept in the food locker on the wall, a precaution against the rats that sometimes rule the hut: make sure you use the locker to store your food.

Ferry pick-ups from Echo Point are only possible if arranged and paid for in advance (see ferry details at the end of Stage 6). There are decent campsites around the hut or on the lake shore.

An unfortunate consequence of even the briefest visit to Echo Point is the likely re-emergence of the catchy '80s pop tune 'Echo Beach'.

Interior of Echo Point Hut

Echo Point Hut to Cynthia Bay, 10.7km, 3–4hr

From Echo Point Hut, cross the creek and continue along the edge of the lake. The track soon rises through lovely sassafras-dominated rainforest to follow a contour about 20m above the lake. The path passes beneath an extensive forest of some of the tallest, straightest myrtle on the track. Around 2.3km from Echo Point Hut cross two curving boardwalks to enter a long stretch of silver wattle and ferns, the ferns pressing forward to crowd the path. ◂

This previously burnt area is an interesting example of succession after fire, the result of a hiker burning off toilet paper in 1976.

Returning to rainforest dotted with enormous tree ferns, a massive **gumtopped stringybark** on the shore indicates the start of a transition to woodland, 2.9km from Echo Point and 7.8km from Cynthia Bay. From here to Cynthia Bay the track slowly becomes drier and broader, often with the fresh smell of eucalypt leaves underfoot.

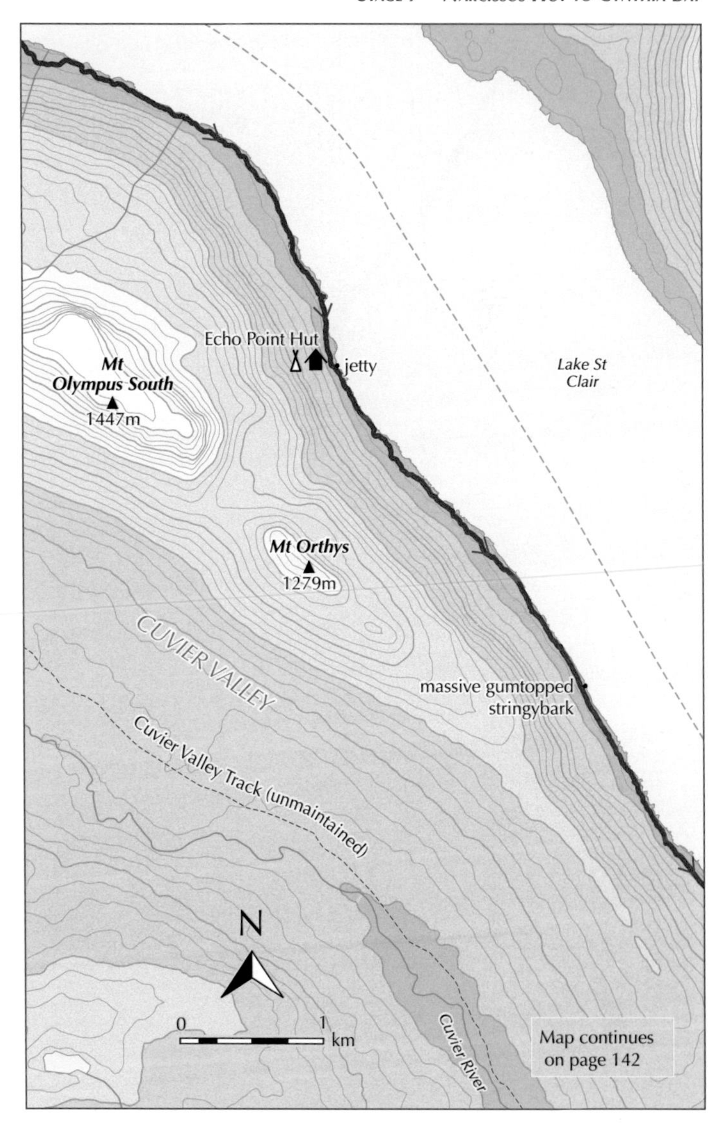
Echo Point Hut
jetty
Mt
Olympus South
1447m
Lake St
Clair
Mt Orthys
1279m
CUVIER VALLEY
massive gumtopped
stringybark
Cuvier Valley Track (unmaintained)
N
0
1
km
Cuvier River
Map continues
on page 142

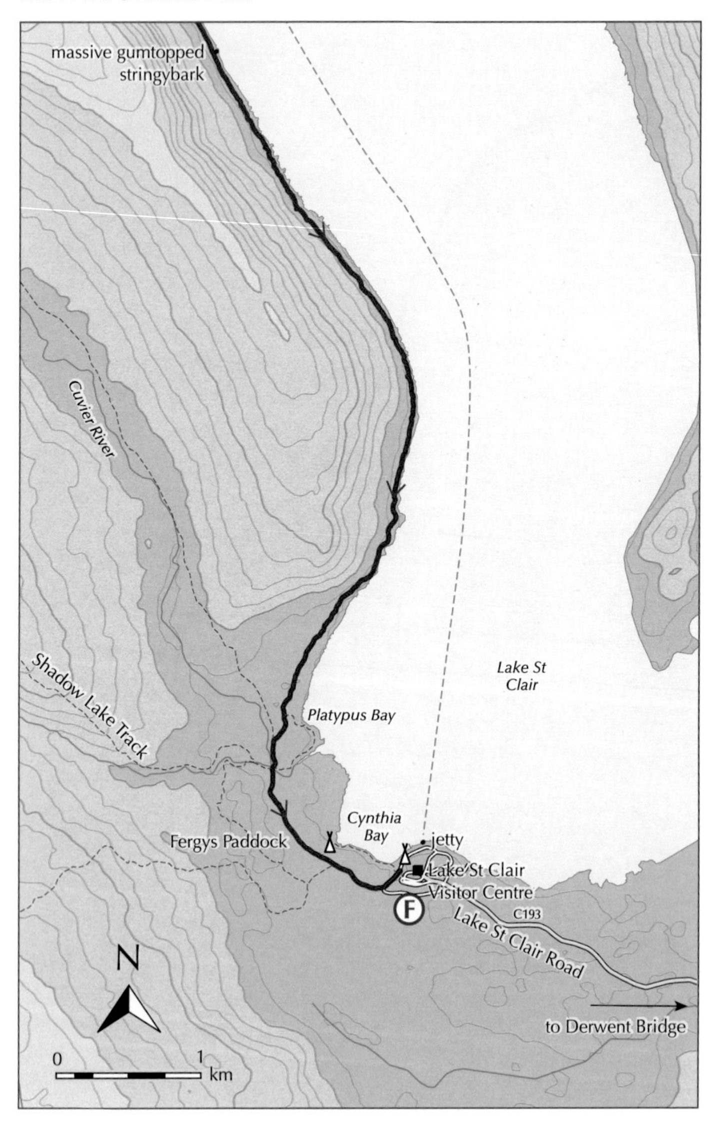

massive gumtopped stringybark
Cuvier River
Shadow Lake Track
Lake St Clair
Platypus Bay
Cynthia Bay
Fergys Paddock
jetty
Lake St Clair Visitor Centre
F
C193
Lake St Clair Road
N
to Derwent Bridge
0
1
km

Pass through tunnels of musk daisybush, a shrub that colonises burnt rainforest with its windblown seed, into more rainforest. At a gully 2.5km from Cynthia Bay, the vegetation abruptly completes the change to a drier, rockier open woodland containing mountain pinkberry, guitarplant and cabbage gums. Some 600 metres later, reach the **junction** with the track to **Platypus Bay** and 200 metres beyond that a second **junction**, where the alternative route from Narcissus Hut via the Cuvier Valley rejoins the Overland.

The track now follows a moraine ridge – a mound deposited by the glaciers that carved this valley and formed Lake St Clair. With the burble of the Cuvier River audible, **Watersmeet** is soon reached, the spot where the Cuvier joins the Hugel River to flow into Lake St Clair. Cross the bridge, a lavish affair after the comparative simplicity of the Overland, the pretty rivers twisting and surging through smooth boulders as they merge. On the other side, follow the signs to the **Lake St Clair Visitor Centre** on a wide gravel track, a logging road from the 1960s built on the moraine ridge. The woodland becomes dominated by regrowth until the junction with **Fergys Paddock** is reached, 660m from the Visitor Centre.

Fergys Paddock, 100m off the main track, is a free camping area for Overlanders. There are good campsites on the flat, sandy ground beside the lake and a toilet among the trees to the north-west.

From the junction with Fergys Paddock the forest becomes dominated by silver banksia. Follow the gravel road until the Visitor Centre appears, a huge, green contemporary structure crowned by an atrium. Beneath the atrium, opposite the information centre, is a booth containing the hikers' deregistration book.

Congratulations and commiserations: your Overland is over.

CYNTHIA BAY

There's not much to Cynthia Bay apart from the brown rangers' houses, the buildings associated with the Lake St Clair Visitor Centre and the various accommodation options of Lake St Clair Lodge. The Visitor Centre incorporates a café/restaurant as well as the information centre, which has interesting displays as well as hiking clothes and books for sale. Within the centre there are also three free showers for walkers (from 10am to 4pm), a payphone and a drinking water tap.

The distant art deco building on the lakeshore to the east is the old pumping station from the hydroelectric scheme, now the exclusive Pumphouse Point resort. If arriving at Cynthia Bay by ferry, turn right from the jetty – the Visitor Centre is 200m along the gravel road. Buses leave from the car park near the information centre.

If you feel like more walking, then there are some good short walks in the Cynthia Bay area, including the Larmairrenemer tabelti Aboriginal cultural walk (approximately 4km, 1.5hr return). You can get to the start of the walk via the lakeshore and Fergys Paddock instead of retracing your steps along the Overland.

For more information on Cynthia Bay and nearby Derwent Bridge, see the Accommodation and facilities at the end of the track section.

Lake St Clair Visitor Centre

PLANT AND ANIMAL GUIDE

Some of Tasmania's endemic species (photos: Alan Fletcher, Dave Watts)

PLANT GUIDE

To aid identification, the plants in the flora section have been arranged into five simplified vegetation communities: alpine and subalpine, buttongrass moorland and heath, eucalypt forest, grassland and rainforest. Some species occur in more than one community, but for the sake of brevity have been included only in their most common habitat type. Within these divisions the plants have been ordered from smallest to largest. The flora section contains 47 plants that grow along the track, however more than 450 species are found within the national park.

Keep in mind that flowering times can vary and all plants in the park are fully protected. Endemic species (those only found in Tasmania) are marked with an '(e)'. Abbreviations are used for other territories and countries: Australian Capital Territory (ACT), New South Wales (NSW), Victoria (Vic), Queensland (Qld), South Australia (SA) and New Zealand (NZ).

ALPINE AND SUBALPINE

About 10 per cent of Tasmania can be said to be alpine or subalpine – half of Australia's total alpine area. Unlike the mainland, Tasmania's alpine areas don't have a clear tree line, a distinct altitude at which trees stop growing. Snow peppermints, pencil pine, King Billy pine and deciduous beech continue to grow at high altitudes, albeit in progressively stunted forms, as long as the soil, shelter and moisture make it possible. The alpine area along the Overland Track is the low growing vegetation above about 1200m.

Also unlike the mainland, Tasmania's alpine areas don't have a permanent winter snow cover; snow thaws between falls leaving the ground open to erosion by ice, water and wind. The elements prevent soil accumulating, leaving exposed areas as bare rock, or with the thinnest mantle of soil, often reddish from the large amount of iron and magnesium found in the dolerite rock that forms the mountain peaks.

These tough conditions produce specialised plants: up to 60 per cent of Tasmania's alpine plants are found nowhere else in the world. Having to endure snow, frequent frosts, extreme summer temperature fluctuations, high rainfall and fierce gales has led to many adaptations, including species hugging the ground for warmth and to avoid the wind, flexibility – bending rather than breaking under a load of snow – and small leathery leaves to protect the plants from damage from blasting winds and ice.

Taller shrubs are found only in the lee of rocks, where some soil can accumulate and there's a little more warmth and shelter from the abrasive winds.

Creeping pine (e)

Microcachrys tetragona

A prostrate conifer with square plait-like stems.

Size: Prostrate, although mature stems are often raised.

Foliage: Tiny, overlapping, in four rows giving stems a square appearance like plaiting.

Fruit: Cones form at end of branches. Male cone very small, female cone fleshy and red when ripe, to 1cm. Autumn.

Habitat/Distribution: Alpine areas in the north, west and south of Tasmania, 1000–1500m.

Snow cushionplant

Donatia novae-zelandiae

There are seven species of cushion-plant in Tasmania, each a low, rounded mound comprising hundreds of small, tightly packed plants. Their shape protects them from the fierce winds and allows them to store enough warmth and water to survive freezing winter conditions.

Size: Numerous tiny plants form a dark-green, low, hard mound up to 1m in diameter.

Flowers: Star-shaped white flowers with five petals, 5mm across, often appearing half-open, with petals pointing upwards. Summer.

Foliage: Tiny, pointed, fleshy, densely packed with white hairs at leaf-base.

Fruit: Small cups with loose seeds spread by rain.

Habitat/Distribution: Exposed mountain summits and plateaus. Also NZ.

Snow everlasting (e)
Helichrysum milliganii

Elegant mountain daisy with papery 'petals'.

Size: Height: 5–15cm. Width: 2–5cm.

Flowers: Single white flower head on woolly stem, 2–3cm across, centre golden yellow. Petals are actually modified leaves called 'bracts', which, like all everlastings, feel dry and papery. Mid to late summer.

Foliage: Fleshy, pointed bright-green leaves from compact basal rosette.

Fruit: Like a dandelion; each seed attached to a tiny feathery parachute for dispersal by wind.

Habitat/Distribution: Rocky outcrops and alpine grasslands in Tasmania's western and central mountains.

Pineapple grass (e)
Astelia alpina var. alpina

An apt common name, as the stiff, mat-forming plants are tufted like a pineapple. This is a common plant on the Overland's damp, mountain moors.

Size: Height: 1–15cm. Width: 1–60cm.

Flowers: Small, greenish, in short spikes hidden among leaves. February–March.

Foliage: Sword-shaped, grey-green above, silvery or brown below, stiff, channelled, 6–40cm long.

Fruit: Red, oval berries, about 1cm long.

Habitat/Distribution: Widespread in Tasmania's mountain areas.

Orange everlasting
Xerochrysum subundulatum

A perennial daisy that can form large clumps.

Size: Height: 10–30cm.

Flowers: Bright gold–orange, 3–4cm in diameter with papery petal-like bracts (bracts are actually modified leaves). January–March.

Foliage: Light-green, rough, narrow, spoon-shaped, about 8cm long.

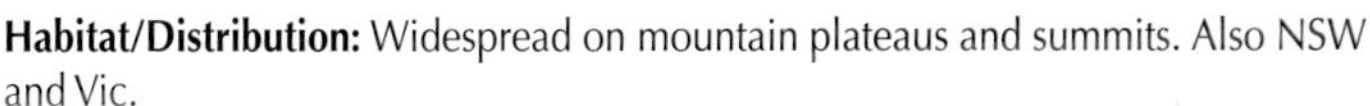

Habitat/Distribution: Widespread on mountain plateaus and summits. Also NSW and Vic.

Broadleaf boronia
Boronia rhomboidea

The leaves of this plant have a pleasant smell when crushed.

Size: Height: 10–30cm. Width: 0.5–1m.

Flowers: White–pink, four petals. Buds deep pink–red. Summer.

Foliage: Green with reddish edges, rounded, to 1cm across, stalkless, held semi-erect on stems. Aromatic.

Fruit: Small capsule.

Habitat/Distribution: Exposed alpine areas to 1200m. Also NSW.

Mountain rocket (e)
Bellendena montana

This small distinctive shrub is spectacular twice a year: once over summer when its feathery flowers are in bloom and then again in late summer–autumn when its brilliant orange–red fruits form.

Size: Height: 10–60cm. Width: 1–2m.

Flowers: Pyramid of small white–pale pink flowers on the end of long stem well above the level of the leaves. Summer.

Foliage: Green, leathery, 2–4cm, held upwards with tips either rounded or in three blunt lobes.

Fruit: Flattened oval papery sacs in vivid red, yellow or orange, hanging from raised stems.

Habitat/Distribution: Common in Tasmania's mountain areas.

Silky milligania (e)
Milligania densiflora

Climb nearly any of the peaks along the Overland, such as Cradle Mountain, Mt Ossa or The Acropolis, and you'll see carpets of these lilies near the top, thriving among the fallen rock.

Size: Height: 15–75cm.

Flowers: Small, numerous, white–cream, sometimes reddish in centre, tubular with six widely spread petals, held on thick, densely hairy flower stems 20–75cm long. Late spring–early summer.

Foliage: Strap-like, 15–30cm long, with fine hairs on edges and midrib.

Fruit: Capsule.

Habitat/Distribution: Tasmania's moist alpine slopes and rocky banks.

Spreading cheeseberry (e)
Cyathodes straminea

Cheeseberries get their name from their fleshy fruits which resemble small Edam cheeses.

Size: Height: 0.25–1m. Width: 0.3–0.75m.

Flowers: White, tubular, crowded towards ends of branches with an unpleasant smell. Summer.

Foliage: Blunt, glossy green, 5–15mm, paler beneath with clearly defined parallel veins.

Fruit: Flattened, red, fleshy, containing one seed.

Habitat/Distribution: Common in alpine heaths above 1100m.

Christmas bells (e)
Blandfordia punicea

Another Christmas present for Overlanders: the spectacular bell-shaped flowers of this lily are out in early summer.

Size: Height: 0.5–1.0m. Width: 20–40cm.

Flowers: Brilliant orange–red, bell-shaped, up to 5cm long, with bright yellow tips. Clusters of flowers hang downwards on short stalks from a long, erect stem. Early summer.

Foliage: Long, tough, strap-like, 15–45cm, tufted at base. Fine serrations on leaf edges.

Fruit: Long, triangular pod held upright on stem.

Habitat/Distribution: Rocky low-nutrient slopes.

Central lemon boronia (e)

Boronia citriodora subsp. citriodora

As both the common and Latin names indicate, the leaves of this common Overland shrub have a strong lemony smell.

Size: Height: 0.5–1m. Width: 0.5–1m.

Flowers: Four, pointed, white–pink petals. Buds are often a deeper pink. December–March.

Foliage: Bright green, lance-shaped, crowded, leathery leaves divided into 5 or 7 leaflets, 3–8mm long. Aromatic.

Fruit: Small capsule.

Habitat/Distribution: Common in heathlands and woodlands of Tasmania's Central Highlands.

Alpine heathmyrtle

Baeckea gunniana

A shrub with tiny flowers and leaves that takes a prostrate form on exposed alpine sites. Foliage has a lemony-eucalyptus smell when crushed.

Size: Height: prostrate–1.5m. Width: 0.5–2m.

Flowers: Small, white, five-petalled 2–5mm in diameter, often abundant. Summer.

Foliage: Tiny, crowded, thick, 2–6mm long. Aromatic.

Fruit: Capsule.

Habitat/Distribution: Common in moist areas above 800m. Also NSW and Vic.

Revolute orites (e)
Orites revolutus

'Revolute' and 'revolutus' refer to this common alpine shrub's tightly rolled leaves.

Size: Height: 1–2m. Width: 0.5–1m.

Flowers: Creamy white, 'spidery', held in spikes up to 4cm long at the ends of branches. Early summer.

Foliage: Linear, leathery, edges curved hiding the rusty hairs on the underside, 1–2cm long.

Fruit: Pod-like, opening on one side, 1cm long, covered in rusty hair. Old pods persist on plant.

Habitat/Distribution: Common on Tasmania's mountains and mountain plateaus.

Mountain pinkberry (e)
Leptecophylla juniperina subsp. parvifolia

This small, wiry shrub calls attention to itself with its bright red berries, often found on the plant year-round. The berries are a favourite food for black currawongs and the regurgitated remains of their berry feasts are often seen along the track, the process aiding seed dispersal. There are three subspecies in Tasmania.

Size: Height: 0.5–1.5m. Width: 0.5–1m.

Flowers: White, small, tubular, single flowers in junction of leaves. September–December.

Foliage: Needle-like, pale beneath, about 6mm long with a sharp point.

Fruit: Pale pink to bright red spherical berry, about 6mm in diameter.

Habitat/Distribution: Common subalpine and alpine plant.

Scoparia (e)
Richea scoparia

Spectacular summer flowers make this one of the best-known plants along the track. *Richea gunnii* looks similar but is found mostly on wet sites, has downturned leaves and does not retain old leaves.

Size: Height: 0.5–3m. Width: 1–2m.

Flowers: 4–12cm tall flower-spikes form at ends of branches. Fused petals form a cap, which falls off when the flower is ready to be fertilised. Flowers come in a variety of colours – white, yellow, orange, pink and red – and resemble swollen grains of rice. Summer.

Foliage: Green, hard, sharply pointed and densely crowded, 2–6cm long, overlapping around the stem with dead leaves remaining on plant for several years.

Fruit: Capsule.

Habitat/Distribution: Very common in Tasmania's subalpine to alpine areas.

Purple cheeseberry (e)
Cyathodes glauca

The three species of Cyathodes in Tasmania– *C. glauca*, *C. platystoma* and *C. straminea* – occur nowhere else in the world.

Size: Height: 0.6–3m. Width: 1–2m.

Flowers: White, slightly hairy tubular flowers, 6–10mm long, crowded towards ends of branches. Summer.

Foliage: Leaves stiff, pointed, glossy green, 1.5–3cm, paler beneath with clearly defined parallel veins.

Fruit: Persists most of the year. A flattened drupe about 1cm across, white, pink or purple, most commonly mauve on the Overland.

Habitat/Distribution: Common on wet hillsides below 1100m.

Pandani (e)
Richea pandanifolia subsp. pandanifolia

Resembling a palm and often growing in groves, the shaggy-headed pandani can reach 10m tall within rainforest.

Size: Height: 1–10m. Width: 1–3m.

Flowers: Cascade of pink–red flowers tucked among base of leaves. As with other Richea species, the petals form caps. Late spring–summer.

Foliage: Tough, tapering, to 1.5m, with fine teeth at margins. Leaves' tips twist as they dry off. Dead leaves form a 'skirt' covering the trunk beneath the green crown. These dry leaves were formerly used to start campfires.

Fruit: Capsule.

Habitat/Distribution: Open, moist slopes, subalpine to 1500m, often growing in groves.

Dwarf pine (e)
Diselma archeri

Depending on altitude and the amount of shelter, the dwarf pine can have a range of forms, from a small tree to a prostrate shrub. Most commonly it's a small, dense shrub with drooping growth-tips.

Size: Height: 0.5–5m. Width: 1–1.4m

Foliage: Scale-like, 2–3mm long, tightly overlapping like braiding.

Fruit: Male and female cones on separate plants. Male cones among the smallest of any conifer, green ripening to brown, 2–3mm.

Habitat/Distribution: Widespread in the moist soils of Tasmania's southern and western mountains from 1000–1400m.

Deciduous beech (e)
Nothofagus gunnii

In late April the green leaves of Australia's only autumn deciduous tree turn golden yellow and sometimes deep red before being shed. This unusual adaptation dates back to Gondwana when long, dark winters meant there was little sunlight for photosynthesis, effectively putting the trees into hibernation until spring.

Size: Height: 1.5–5m. Width: 1.5–2m.

Flowers: Small, inconspicuous, pale brown. Male and female flowers on same tree. Summer.

Foliage: Bright-green, oval–round, scalloped edges, 4–10mm across with a distinctly pleated, 'crinkle- cut' appearance. No leaves from late autumn–winter.

Fruit: Small woody nut, 8mm long.

Bark: Grey.

Habitat/Distribution: Occurs in isolated patches on sheltered slopes in western and central Tasmania from 800–1400m.

BUTTONGRASS MOORLAND AND HEATH

Buttongrass moorland covers about 15 per cent of Tasmania and it's the tannins and oils in buttongrass that give many western Tasmanian rivers and lakes their characteristic tea colour. The low growing sedges and heaths of buttongrass moorland occur on poorly drained, low-nutrient plains with an annual rainfall above 1000mm, high humidity, low temperatures and low evaporation. These conditions allow the formation of peat – an accumulation of organic material from dead plants and animals.

Buttongrass moorland is extremely flammable. Peat fires can smoulder undetected for months before erupting into flames. Regular burning by Aboriginal people was important to maintain the moorlands, as without fire they would gradually fill with shrubs and convert to rainforest.

Spreading guineaflower
Hibbertia procumbens

One of the most common plants on the Overland, this ground-hugging species forms dense mats at the edge of the track. It occurs in many vegetation communities.

Size: Prostrate, spreading in mats to 1m across.

Flowers: Large golden yellow five-petalled flowers, about 2.5cm in diameter. Late spring–summer.

Foliage: Small, bright-green, 5–15mm long, fleshy, in bundles on narrow, wiry stems.

Fruit: Brown and papery.

Habitat/Distribution: Sunny areas on bare ground, common in heathland and moorland. Also Vic.

Alpine coralfern
Gleichenia alpina

The most common fern along the track, forming low, dense, green mats, often tinged with orange new growth in the warmer months.

Size: Height: 15–25cm.

Foliage: Fronds divided into many 'leaflets' each comprising tiny bubbles like rows of miniature beads. New growth is orange.

Fruit: Reproduction via spores held beneath each bead-like pouch.

Habitat/Distribution: Common on mountain moors. Also NZ.

Buttongrass
Gymnoschoenus sphaerocephalus

One of the signature species of the Overland, you'll see large groups of this distinctive coppery-green tussock on nearly every leg of your walk. Their common name comes from the round 'button-like' flower heads held on narrow stalks above the plant.

Size: Height: 0.5–1m. Width: 0.5–1m.

Flowers: Tiny, white, forming spherical flower heads 1.5–2cm in diameter on long, thin stalks held above tussock. Summer.

Foliage: Bright green blades with gold, yellow and bronze, arching out from centre of clump, to 60cm long, smooth and rigid.

Fruit: 4mm long nut.

Habitat/Distribution: Mostly in the western half of Tasmania in open areas with high rainfall and poor soils. Also NSW, Vic., Qld and SA.

Wiry bauera
Bauera rubioides

Sprawling wiry shrub with long spreading branches. Bauera is common in damp, shaded areas.

Size: Height: 0.5–2m. Width: 1–2m.

Flowers: Usually white, sometimes pink, 1.5–2cm across, hanging downwards on slender stalks from near ends of branches. Number of petals varies from five to nine, but commonly five or six. Anthers yellow. September–February but also sporadically throughout the year.

Foliage: Small, dark-green leaves appearing as a whorl of six around stem (although, actually, they are two tri-lobed leaves).

Fruit: Capsule.

Habitat/Distribution: Abundant in damp, sheltered areas to 1000m (although not rainforest). Also NSW, Vic., Qld and SA.

Golden shaggypea
Oxylobium ellipticum

This shrub is also sometimes known as 'golden rosemary'.

Size: Height: 1–2.5m. Width: 1–2m.

Flowers: Clusters of orange-yellow pea flowers at ends of branches. Dead flowers may persist on plant. Early summer.

Foliage: Elliptical, dull green leathery leaves 1–4cm long with obvious central vein and rolled edges, often slightly hairy beneath. While leaf tips are generally blunt they may have a tiny pointed tip.

Fruit: Brown, hairy, 7mm-long, pointed pod.

Habitat/Distribution: Moist, rocky spots in woodland and alpine areas in the north and north-west of Tasmania. Also NSW, Vic. and Qld.

Mountain geebung (e)
Persoonia gunnii var. gunnii

The fleshy fruit of the geebung is tempting to animals, which consume it and disperse the seed.

Size: Height: 1–3m. Width: 1.5–3m.

Flowers: Cream, trumpet-like, about 15mm long, with a strong odour. December–April.

Foliage: Flat, leathery, bent to curve upwards, to 6cm long, widest towards tip, no veins visible.

Fruit: Ovoid, fleshy, green turning purple, about 1cm long, often mature at the same time as next season's flowers.

Habitat/Distribution: Slopes of central and western mountains.

Swamp honeymyrtle
Melaleuca squamea

There are six native species of Melaleuca in Tasmania. Melaleucas are also sometimes known as 'paperbarks' as some species have pale, papery bark.

Size: Height: 1–3m. Width: 1–2m.

Flowers: White or mauve pompom-like tufts at ends of branches. Late spring–summer.

Foliage: Hairy, crowded, arranged alternately around stem, with soft-pointed tips curved back towards branch, 4–8mm long.

Fruit: Clusters of persistent woody stem-clasping capsules.

Habitat/Distribution: Common in wet heaths, sea level to 1500m. Also NSW, Vic. and SA.

EUCALYPT FOREST

Eucalypt forests have the greatest diversity of plants and animals of any Tasmanian vegetation community. There are five main species of eucalypt on the Overland, which act as important nesting and hollow sites for birds and mammals. Eucalypts are the successors of the more primitive Gondwanan species, their adaptations to fire and drought making them well suited to Australian conditions.

Apart from the snow peppermint, which can tolerate very high altitudes, most eucalypts grow in sheltered valleys on the more fertile well-drained mineral soils. Along the Narcissus Valley and near Cynthia Bay eucalypts grow on glacial moraines.

Guitarplant (e)

Lomatia tinctoria

The catchy name is derived from the shape of the plant's fruit. The guitarplant has a close relative, the mountain guitarplant, *Lomatia polymorpha,* which is also found on the Overland. *Lomatia polymorpha* can be distinguished from *Lomatia tinctoria* by the absence of divided leaves and its more compact flower spike.

Size: Height: 0.5–2m. Width: 0.5–1m.

Flowers: Small white–cream, pleasant smelling, long-stalked, forming loose spikes at end of branches. January.

Foliage: Dark-green, shape varies but usually divided into long slender lobes 1–4cm long. New growth reddish.

Fruit: Dry, woody, opening along one side into a guitar shape (although it actually more closely resembles a lute).

Habitat/Distribution: Tolerates a range of conditions to 1000m.

Silver banksia

Banksia marginata

The long, golden, cob-flowers of this common banksia are an important source of nectar for birds.

Size: Height: 2–9m. Width: 2–6m.

Flowers: Lemon yellow to gold cylindrical flower heads, 5–10cm long. Cones retained on tree, becoming grey with age. November–April.

Foliage: Dark-green above, silvery below, prominent midrib, edges smooth or notched, particularly at tips.

Fruit: Woody pod partly embedded in cone.

Bark: Grey.

Habitat/Distribution: Common on wide variety of sites, preferring heaths and woodland. Also NSW, Vic., SA and ACT.

Cider gum (e)

Eucalyptus gunnii subsp. gunnii

Aboriginal people and early settlers made deep cuts in the bark of this tree in early summer to tap the sap which could be fermented to make a drink similar to apple cider. Alpine cider gum, *Eucalyptus archeri*, looks similar but has glossy green leaves.

Size: Height: 8–25m. Width: 6–15m.

Flowers: White–cream, 1.5cm across, in groups of three. Summer.

Foliage: Juvenile: waxy grey-green, round, stem-clasping. Adult: grey-green, leathery, 5–8cm long, with pointed tip.

Buds: In threes, with a small point on rounded cap.

Fruit: Cylindrical capsules, top depressed.

Bark: Sometimes grey rough bark on lower trunks of older trees, smooth above and on branches, cream with pinkish-grey and olive-tan.

Habitat/Distribution: Central highlands 800–1100m, often in poorly drained frost-prone depressions.

Silver wattle

Acacia dealbata subsp. dealbata

Often appearing in groves, silver wattles frequently colonise areas of forest that have been disturbed by a fallen tree or fire. It can be shrubby on drier sites or a tall tree in moist valleys, their bright yellow flowers appearing as beacons on a gloomy winter's day.

Size: Height: 3–30m. Width: 3–15m.

Flowers: Bright yellow balls, numerous, 5–6mm diameter, in sprays of 25–30. July–October.

Foliage: Blue-green, feathery, twice divided, to 13cm long.

Fruit: Purplish-brown oblong pod 5–8cm long.

Bark: Grey, smooth, mottled.

Habitat/Distribution: Widespread in damp forest, along streams, also drier woodland. Also NSW and Vic.

Cabbage gum

Eucalyptus pauciflora subsp. pauciflora

Eucalyptus pauciflora is commonly known as 'snow gum' on the mainland.

Size: Height: 6–30m. Width: 3–4m.

Flowers: White–cream, to 1.5cm across, in clusters of 7–12. Summer.

Foliage: Juvenile: dull blue-green, leathery, 3–8cm wide, up to 14cm long. Adult: glossy green, leathery, 10–18cm long, with veins almost parallel to midrib. Sometimes with a hooked leaf-tip like snow peppermint.

Buds: Club-shaped, in clusters of 5–15.

Fruit: Bell-shaped, thick-rimmed capsules about 1cm across, with top level with rim. Usually three valves.

Bark: Smooth, yellow and white streaked with browny-red, pink or even olive.

Habitat/Distribution: Central and eastern Tasmania from alpine to lowlands. Also NSW and Vic.

Snow peppermint (e)
Eucalyptus coccifera

Appears as a tall tree with a straight trunk in sheltered positions with good soil, and as a gnarled shrub on sites exposed to wind and snow.

Size: Height: 2–40m. Width: 3–10m.

Flowers: White, in clusters of 3 to about 15. Late spring–summer.

Foliage: Juvenile: pale grey-green, oval, with a small point at tip, often on crimson stems. Adult: green to grey-blue, often held erect, oblong, relatively small, to 8cm long, sometimes with a crimson hooked tip.

Buds: Long, ribbed, often light bluish-green with a wrinkled cap, in clusters of 7–15.

Fruit: Cup-shaped capsules, often waxy grey-blue, about 1cm wide, topped with a flat disc level with rim.

Bark: Smooth, streaked with white, cream, grey and pink. Older trees may have rough bark around base.

Habitat/Distribution: Common on exposed mountain tops and plateaus, 800–1300m, in south-east Tasmania and Central Plateau.

Alpine yellow gum (e)
Eucalyptus subcrenulata

Often growing among snow peppermints, the alpine yellow gum can also tolerate wetter soils, sometimes appearing in rainforest where it grows tall and straight.

Size: Height: 6–55m. Width: 8–15m.

Flowers: White, 1.5cm across, in clusters of 3. Summer.

Foliage: Juvenile: glossy green, leathery, round, with faintly scalloped edges, to 6cm long, often persisting on large trees. Adult: glossy green, leathery, 3–8cm long, with faintly scalloped edges.

Buds: Short, stout, in clusters of 3.

Fruit: Bell-shaped, ribbed, green-brown capsules, top slightly protruding.

Bark: Smooth, often shiny and colourful. Sheds old brown bark to reveal streaks of grey, cream, olive green and yellow-orange.

Habitat/Distribution: Central Plateau and southern mountains, usually on sloping areas around valleys, 700–1100m.

Gumtopped stringybark (e)
Eucalyptus delegatensis subsp. tasmaniensis

Look out for this eucalypt's large, red-tinted leaves along the track.

Size: Height: 20–90m. Width: 10–30m.

Flowers: White, up to 1.5cm wide, clusters of 7–15, usually 11. January.

Foliage: Juvenile: blue-grey, elliptical, asymmetrical (joining the stem unevenly), often reddish. Adult: dull blue-green, 8–16cm long, also asymmetrical.

Buds: Relatively slender, club-shaped, in clusters of 7–15.

Fruit: Pear-shaped capsules on small stalks, to 1.5cm wide, top slightly depressed.

Bark: Rough, fibrous, grey-brown on most of trunk, upper trunk and branches smooth cream–grey.

Habitat/Distribution: Common at altitudes from 400–900m. While subspecies *tasmaniensis* is found only in Tasmania, the species *delegantensis* can be found in NSW and Vic.

GRASSLAND

Grassland tends to occur where the soils are deep, fertile and not too rocky – not very often in Cradle Mountain–Lake St Clair National Park. Pockets of grassland are sometimes found in depressions where other plants can't survive the severe frosts.

Mountain bluebell (e)
Wahlenbergia saxicola

Wahlenbergia's blue flowers seem too large for their slender stems.

Size: Height: 3–9cm.

Flowers: Pale to sky blue on ends of slender stems, 4–5 petals, about 2cm in diameter. Summer.

Foliage: Finely toothed, elliptical, 1–3cm long in basal rosette.

Fruit: Capsule.

Habitat/Distribution: Grassy and rocky areas in eastern mountains.

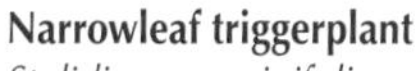

Narrowleaf triggerplant
Stylidium graminifolium

Triggerplants have developed a unique method to ensure pollination. Insects probing for nectar trigger a tiny hammer held above the flower which flicks towards the flower's centre, depositing pollen on the insect's back or picking up any pollen previously deposited. The narrowleaf triggerplant is one of the most widely distributed triggerplant species in Australia.

Size: Height: 20–60cm. Width: 20–30cm.

Flowers: A long spike with numerous small, deep pink butterfly-shaped flowers. October–February.

Foliage: Narrow, less than 4mm wide, green-grey, grass-like, 5–20cm long, from basal rosette.

Fruit: Small capsule.

Habitat/Distribution: Common in low-nutrient soils such as rocky areas and peat. Also NSW, Vic., Qld and SA.

RAINFOREST

Tasmania has the largest areas of cool temperate rainforest in Australia, covering about 10 per cent of the state, mostly in the west. Cool temperate rainforest is different from rainforest found in warmer areas as it contains no palms, few vines, is less diverse and the trees aren't usually buttressed.

Most of the rainforest along the track is termed 'myrtle' rainforest as myrtle beech is the dominant rainforest tree. There's usually a thick canopy layer of myrtle beneath which relatively few species can grow. Where a break in the canopy allows in light, other species such as leatherwood, celerytop pine and sassafras can get a start, with King Billy pines found in higher elevation rainforest. These species can also get a start when the soil is poor, as poor soils usually mean a thinner myrtle canopy. Where the soil is richer and deeper the myrtles grow huge, shading out competing plants, leaving only mosses, lichens and liverworts below. The trunks of the myrtle are particularly abundant in these species, with over 150 types identified.

The temperature in the rainforest tends to be relatively constant as it's shielded from the sun and protected against the wind. Walking in myrtle rainforest can be slow as the path is invariably wet, rocky and root-tangled.

Mother shieldfern

Polystichum proliferum

A beautiful fern, with its arching fronds forming a raised rosette. The common name derives from the tiny plants that develop at the tips of mature fronds – when the fronds droop to the ground these plants take root to form new ferns. Mature plants can develop a short 'trunk' to 10cm thick.

Size: Height: 0.5–1.5m. Width: 0.5–1.5m.

Foliage: Bright light-green when young, dark-green when mature, leathery, with hairy midrib. Fronds to 1m long, first erect then arching, twice divided, often bearing new plants near tip.

Fruit: Propagates by spores or new plants on frond-tips.

Habitat/Distribution: Common in moist forest understorey, also in alpine rockeries. Also NSW and Vic.

Cutting grass

Gahnia grandis

A huge grass-like tussock with sharply serrated leaves.

Size: Height: 1.5–3.0m. Width: 1.5–3.0m.

Flowers: Light brown–black plume-like flower heads 50–100cm long, with small, yellow flowering parts on stout stems, 1.5–3m high. November–January.

Foliage: Long, narrow strap-like leaves to 2m long, rough, flat, with very sharp edges. Leaves initially erect then bend over further from the clump.

Fruit: Small, bright orange-brown nuts.

Habitat/Distribution: Moist–wet areas, often in clearings. Also NSW and Vic.

Mountain pepper

Tasmannia lanceolata

This plant has become a fairly common bush food, its leaves and fruit sold in supermarkets as a peppery spice. Taste a leaf, but look out – they're hot!

Size: Height: 2–5m. Width: 1.5–3m.

Flowers: Creamy, in clusters, about 1cm across, male and female on separate plants. October–December.

Foliage: Glossy dark-green above, paler green beneath, thick, hairless, lance-shaped, smooth edges, prominent midrib, length variable 3–13cm. Young stems and leaf stalks are bright red.

Fruit: Glossy purple–black, round, about 5mm diameter.

Bark: Smooth, brownish-grey.

Habitat/Distribution: Widespread in high rainfall areas, particularly in rainforest and wet eucalypt forest, common in subalpine woodlands and heath. Also NSW, Vic. and ACT.

Woolly tea-tree
Leptospermum lanigerum

A very common species along the track, often in dense stands fringing rainforest.

Size: Height: 2–5m. Width: 1–3m.

Flowers: Single, white, 1.5cm in diameter, numerous. Late spring–summer, also sporadically throughout the year.

Foliage: Dull green-blue, silky/hairy (that is, woolly), particularly beneath, oblong–oval shaped, 1–1.5cm long.

Fruit: Young capsules silky/hairy, becoming woody, 7–9mm across. Persist on branches.

Bark: Grey, in long, thin paper-like strips.

Habitat/Distribution: Moist areas from riverbanks to rainforest. Also NSW, Vic. and SA.

Tasmanian waratah (e)
Telopea truncata

The pin-up plant of the Overland, the waratah is known as the Christmas decoration of the bush for its striking crimson flower heads on display at that time of the year. It can grow as a tree on favourable sites, but is more commonly seen as a shrub.

Size: Height: 2–8m. Width: 1–2m.

Flowers: Deep red, spidery clusters on ends of branches, 5–8cm across, comprising 15–20 flowers. Late spring–early summer.

Foliage: Variable, dark-green above, paler below, 5–15cm long, with slightly rolled edges.

Fruit: Persistent, brown, banana-shaped pod, 5–8cm long opening when mature to reveal numerous winged seeds.

Habitat/Distribution: Widespread in highland forest, including rainforest, to 1200m.

Pencil pine (e)

Athrotaxis cupressoides

The most ancient pencil pines are thought to be about 2000 years old. It can be distinguished from King Billy pine, which grows in more sheltered forest and has less densely packed leaves. Occasionally hybridises with King Billy pine to produce *Athrotaxis x laxifolia*.

Size: Height: 5–20m. Width: 2–6m.

Foliage: Leaves resemble scales. Olive green, 2–4mm long, blunt tipped, tightly overlapping the branchlets.

Fruit: Spherical cones, green ripening brown and woody, 10mm across.

Bark: Grey-brown, fibrous and furrowed.

Habitat/Distribution: Western and central Tasmania, occasionally in montane rainforest, more commonly along creek and lake edges, from 700–1500m.

Celerytop pine (e)

Phyllocladus aspleniifolius

The celerytop pine's distinctive diamond-shaped 'leaves' are actually flattened stems, thought to be an adaptation to the low light beneath the rainforest canopy. They resemble celery leaves, hence the common name. The conical trees with their horizontally-held branches can be up to 800 years old.

Size: Height: 6–20m. Width: 2–4m.

Foliage: Bright green modified stems, thick, leathery and diamond shaped, 3–8cm long.

Fruit: Fleshy red and white fruits holding a black seed.

Bark: Smooth, grey.

Habitat/Distribution: Widespread in rainforest and wet eucalypt forest to 1000m, mostly in the west of the state.

Leatherwood (e)
Eucryphia lucida

The source of Tasmania's prized leatherwood honey, this rainforest tree can be a spectacular mass of large white flowers in summer.

Size: Height: 6–30m. Width: 2–3m.

Flowers: White, to 4cm in diameter, with four large, rounded petals. The sweet-smelling flowers are found near the ends of the branches in leaf junctions. Summer.

Foliage: Leathery, glossy green above, pale below, 3–4cm long, blunt tipped.

Fruit: Elongated capsule.

Bark: Smooth.

Habitat/Distribution: Common in western Tasmania's moist rainforest.

King Billy pine (e)
Athrotaxis selaginoides

Mature trees can be over 1000 years old with girths greater than two metres. Believed to be named after William Lanney, said to be the last full-blooded male Aboriginal Tasmanian. Like pencil pines they are conical and grow only a few millimetres per year. In the last century alone fire has reduced the population of King Billy pine by a third.

Size: Height: 15–40m. Width: 2–5m.

Foliage: Bright green thick curving needles to 12mm long, loosely overlapping.

Fruit: Spherical cones, green ripening brown, 15mm across at the ends of branchlets.

Bark: Reddish, deeply fibrous and furrowed.

Habitat/Distribution: Rainforests of western and central Tasmania, mostly at higher altitudes. Sometimes isolated plants extend into alpine areas as shrubs.

Sassafras

Atherosperma moschatum subsp. moschatum

A tall rainforest tree with a distinctive conical shape, the sassafras's branches are held almost horizontally to maximise the light on its serrated leaves. Its leaves have a distinctive nutmeg fragrance.

Size: Height: 10–45m. Width: 4–7m.

Flowers: Separate male and female flowers on the same or different tree. Male flowers about 2cm in diameter, female flowers smaller and less showy, both hang facing downwards. Early spring.

Foliage: Aromatic leaves in opposite pairs, shiny dark-green above, whiteish beneath, 4–9cm long, mostly with serrated edges.

Fruit: A hard green capsule opening to release feathery seeds.

Bark: Smooth and pale grey. The bark was used to make bush tea and sold in England as a tonic drink.

Habitat/Distribution: Common in rainforest. Also NSW and Vic.

Myrtle beech

Nothofagus cunninghamii

The dominant tree of the rainforest, mature myrtles can form a dense canopy, with only moss and ferns beneath. An orange golf-ball-like fungus, myrtle orange (*Cyttaria gunnii*), often grows on the trees.

Size: Height: 2–50m. Width: 2–15m.

Flowers: Inconspicuous brown flowers on new growth. Separate male and female flowers on same tree. Late spring–summer.

Foliage: Small, dark-green, heart-shaped, 1–1.5cm, finely toothed on edges. Fresh spring growth can be bright green, red or orange.

Fruit: Small, winged nut.

Bark: Scaly, dark brown, lower trunk often covered in an amazing collection of mosses, lichens and liverworts.

Habitat/Distribution: Very common rainforest species along the track. Stunted forms found at higher altitudes. Also found in Vic.

ANIMAL GUIDE

All the mammals and birds in this section are arranged from smallest to largest, so if you see something new you'll roughly know where to look for it. Some species are also found in other countries and territories, which are marked using abbreviations: New South Wales (NSW), Victoria (Vic), Queensland (Qld), South Australia (SA) and New Zealand (NZ). Species marked with an '(e)' are endemic to Tasmania.

MAMMALS

Eastern pygmy-possum

Cercartetus nanus

photo: Dave Watts

During cold Tasmanian winters this possum can enter torpor, lowering its metabolism and reducing its body temperature for days or weeks.

Description: Fawn-grey above, lighter below. Large eyes, big ears and long whiskers. Its furless tail assists in climbing and also stores fat in its base for use in torpor.

Average size and weight: Head and body: 9cm, tail the same length. Average weight: 30g.

Behaviour: Mostly nocturnal and solitary, they're agile climbers, moving from tree to tree to feed. They sometimes emerge on overcast days, but more commonly spend daylight hours sheltering in tree hollows, stumps, abandoned birds' nests or under bark. They've been known to use nooks in huts as safe places to enter torpor.

Diet: Pollen and nectar, especially from banksias, eucalypts and bottlebrushes, collected with their slightly brushy tongue. Also insects and soft fruits.

Habitat: Found in a wide range of habitats, but prefer wet forests and rainforest.

Distribution: South-east Australia. In Tasmania they are mostly found in the wetter forests on the western side of the state. Preyed upon by owls, quolls, Tasmanian devils and feral cats.

Long-tailed mouse (e)
Pseudomys higginsi

photo: Dave Watts

Some of the light footsteps you might hear in the huts at night are likely to be from this cute little fellow. Like most Tasmanians the long-tailed mouse is a great climber – hang your food out of reach. Of the five species of native rodents in Tasmania, the long-tailed mouse is the only one which is endemic.

Description: Dark grey above, paler below with darker fur around the eyes. Its long tail is clearly two-toned, dark grey above and white below. It's the only native mouse whose tail is longer than its body.

Average size and weight: Head and body: 13cm, tail: 16cm. Average weight: 70g.

Behaviour: Active at night and sometimes during the day in winter, they make use of hollow logs or short burrows to sleep. When threatened they use their long hindfeet to leap about randomly.

Diet: Lichen, moss, ferns, seeds, fruit, fungi, insects and spiders.

Habitat: High rainfall areas of rainforest and wet eucalypt forest. Particularly common on subalpine scree.

Distribution: Tasmania, particularly the high rainfall areas in the west of the state. Preyed upon by owls and quolls. Common in favoured habitat.

Ringtail possum

Pseudocheirus peregrinus

photo: Dave Watts

Ringtail possums get their name from the way they carry their tail in a tight coil when not using it for gripping branches or carrying nesting material. Their tails are tapering and white-tipped, distinguishing them from brush-tail possums whose tails are black and bushy. Ringtails are also smaller than brushtails and, unlike brushtails, spend little time on the ground, preferring the safety of the trees. Look for their nests in dense tea-tree thickets.

Description: Fur reddish brown to dark grey above, lighter below. Pale patches below the eyes and ears and a long, white-tipped tail carried in a coil when not in use, furless towards the tip to help it grip branches.

Average size and weight: Head and body: 33cm, tail the same. Average weight: 1kg.

Behaviour: Sleep in a football-sized nest in tree forks or shrubs during the day, woven from twigs, bark, leaves and grass, coming out at night to forage, often leaping from branch to branch. Hikers might become familiar with their night-time call, a soft, high-pitched insect-like twittering.

Diet: Leaves, flowers, fruits. It is one of the few animals that can stomach euca-lypt leaves.

Habitat: Most areas, particularly abundant in areas of tall, dense tea-tree.

Distribution: Right around the eastern seaboard of Australia and south-west Western Australia. Has adapted to urban areas, often lives in house roofs. Common.

Eastern quoll

Dasyurus viverrinus

The eastern quolls' species name *viverrinus* means 'ferret-like'.

Description: Quick and alert, the eastern quoll is the size of a small cat and has a pointy muzzle. They have two colour varieties, fawny-grey or, less commonly, black. Both have white spots studding their fur, but no spots on their tail, one of the features that distinguishes them from spotted-tail quolls.

photo: Dave Watts

Average size and weight: Head and body: 35cm, tail: 23cm. Weight: 1.3kg. Males are usually larger and heavier than females.

Behaviour: Nocturnal, they hunt alone through grassland and among undergrowth. They sleep in short burrows, hollow logs or rock piles. They sometimes utter a low growl when alarmed.

Diet: Eastern quolls hunt mice, rabbits, rats and insects, as well as eating fruit, seeds and grasses. If the opportunity presents itself they will scavenge carrion left by Tasmanian devils.

Habitat: Found in rainforest, heathland and alpine areas, but prefers a mix of grassland and forest.

Distribution: Found throughout most of Tasmania. Listed as endangered due to climate change and feral cat predation. There have been no eastern quoll sightings on the mainland since the 1960s, although a few quolls were recently re-introduced into a NSW national park.

Platypus

Ornithorhynchus anatinus

photo: Dave Watts

When the first specimens of this unique animal were sent to England scientists suspected they were a hoax, stitched together from a range of other creatures. The platypus and the echidna are the only egg-laying mammals in the world. Tasmania's many pristine lakes and rivers offer a genuine opportunity to spot one of these shy animals.

Description: With a streamlined body, webbed feet, a rubbery 'duck' bill and a broad, paddle-like tail they are certainly unusual. Their deep brown fur has two layers: a waterproof outer layer and a grey, woolly underfur that provides effective insulation against Tasmania's cold waters. Males have a venomous spur on each ankle, capable of inflicting a painful wound.

Average size and weight: 55cm long, including tail. Tasmanian platypuses are bigger and heavier than those on the mainland, males averaging 1.7kg. Females are smaller and lighter.

Behaviour: Active dusk to early morning, they are generally solitary, leaving their burrows to forage all night, diving repeatedly, usually for 20–40 seconds. They are most often sighted as they briefly return to the surface to breathe or eat their catch. Platypuses close their eyes, ears and nostrils underwater. They locate their prey by electrical impulses in their bills in a similar manner to sharks; swinging their heads from side-to-side and detecting the faint electrical muscle contractions of their prey.

Diet: Insects, molluscs, small invertebrates, worms and shrimp.

Habitat: Shallow freshwater for easy access to their bottom-dwelling food. They prefer steep, vegetated banks to make their burrows, often among tree roots just above the waterline.

Distribution: Found all down the east coast of Australia, common in streams, slow moving rivers, lakes and even farm dams. Threatened by pollution and waterside clearing. Recently there's concern over a fungal disease which causes ulcers and can lead to death.

Short-beaked echidna

Tachyglossus aculeatus

photo: Dave Watts

Its scientific name *Tachyglossus* means 'fast tongue' – an echidna's tongue can flick in and out 100 times a minute. *Aculeatus* means 'spiny'. When echidnas are disturbed they quickly lower their head and burrow rapidly into the ground, leaving only their spines exposed. On harder ground they will curl into a tight ball, protecting their head and belly. There are five subspecies of short-beaked echidna, including the Tasmanian setosus.

Description: A distinctive animal with a tubular snout, powerful claws and black-tipped straw-coloured spines on its back and sides. Tasmania's cool weather means its echidnas have longer fur than those on the mainland; their sandy–dark brown fur can even be long enough to obscure their spines. Males have a non-venomous spur on their hindfoot.

Average size and weight: Tasmanian echidnas are larger than the mainland and New Guinean varieties. They average 43cm in length and 4kg in weight.

Behaviour: Echidnas are shy animals, moving with a slow, rolling gait. In the day they forage for ants and termites, their snout detecting their prey's tiny electrical signals. Using their strong forefeet, they rip open ant and termite nests, driving their snout among their quarry and capturing them with their long (up to 18cm) sticky tongue. In very cold areas they may hibernate over winter.

Diet: Termites, ants, worms and invertebrates.

Habitat: Short-beaked echidnas are found from deserts to forests. Prefer dry, open country with an abundance of ants and termites. They don't have a permanent home or nest, sleeping under bushes or in hollow logs.

Distribution: Australia's most widespread mammal, short-beaked echidnas are also found in New Guinea. They remain common. Eagles and Tasmanian devils prey on echidnas. They were a favourite food for Aboriginal people.

Brushtail possum
Trichosurus vulpecula

photo: Dave Watts

As Australia's most common species of possum, Overlanders will become familiar with brushtails as they attempt night-time food raids or make hair-raising screeches. The species' name *Trichosurus* means 'furry tailed', one way of distinguishing them from ringtails, which are

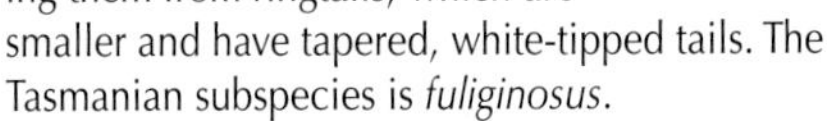
smaller and have tapered, white-tipped tails. The Tasmanian subspecies is *fuliginosus*.

Description: Roughly the size of a cat, their fur ranges in colour from silver-grey to black, or even reddish. Darker coloured possums tend to live in denser, wetter forests. Their tails are black and bushy, relatively short and partly bare along their underside for gripping branches.

Average size and weight: Tasmanian brushtails are larger and furrier than those on the mainland. Head and body are 45cm, tail 30cm, average weight 3.5kg, although in areas with abundant food they can be considerably larger.

Behaviour: Sleep in tree hollows during the day and feed at night. Unlike ringtails, brushtails spend considerable time on the ground. Brushtails make a wide range of sounds: loud rattling nasal coughs, hisses, chattering and hair-raising screeches.

Diet: Mostly leaves, including eucalypt, but also fruit, blossoms, grasses, insects (and muesli bars if given half a chance).

Habitat: Most types, including urban areas. Absent from extensive areas of rainforest and sedgeland.

Distribution: In all mainland states. Common. Main predators are owls and Tasmanian devils.

Other: Brushtails will try all manner of ruses to get to the food they know is inside the huts, including pushing out flywire in the windows. Don't keep your food in your tent: at best you'll get a poor night's sleep as possums attempt to get at it, at worst they'll rip the tent's fabric.

Spotted-tailed quoll

Dasyurus maculatus

photo: Dave Watts

Spotted-tailed quolls are the world's second largest marsupial carnivore (after the Tasmanian devil). Also known as the tiger quoll, perhaps from the deep growling and loud hissing they make during their breeding season around June.

Description: Larger and chunkier than the eastern quoll, spotted-tailed quolls are also distinguished from eastern quolls by having white spots on their tails as well as their bodies. Their fur varies from reddish brown to dark chocolate brown, paler on the belly.

Average size and weight: Head and body 60cm, the tail almost as long. Males average 4kg, females smaller and lighter.

Behaviour: Mostly solitary and nocturnal, they're good climbers, spending about 10 per cent of their time in trees or scampering over logs, keeping balance with their long tails and opposable thumbs on their hind feet. They sometimes emerge during the day to bask in the sun.

Diet: An opportunistic hunter and scavenger, up to 70 per cent of their diet is made up of medium-sized mammals such as gliders, possums, rats, small wallabies and rabbits. They also eat reptiles, eggs, birds, insects and carrion.

Habitat: Found in many types of forest, although more common in the wetter forests and coastal scrub along the north and west coasts of Tasmania. They require habitat with suitable den sites such as rock crevices, caves, burrows and hollow logs. They have territories of up to 500 hectares and can travel more than 6km a night.

Distribution: Endangered on the mainland, vulnerable in Tasmania. Future threatened by land clearing, cats and poison baits used to control wild dogs and stop animals from eating young tree plantations.

Tasmanian devil (e)

Sarcophilus harrisii

photo: Dave Watts

The largest carnivorous marsupial in the world, the Tassie devil is the island's most famous resident. Despite its fearsome name – probably derived from its bloodcurdling screams and its gape-mouthed 'yawn' – devils are shy, cautious animals, so much so that many Tasmanians have never seen one in the wild. They have big teeth and strong jaws for chomping through flesh and bone – a 12kg devil has the biting power of a 50kg dog. In its scientific name *Sarcophilus*, 'sarco' relates to flesh and 'phil' to love – a reference to its love of a good meaty feed.

Description: A stumpy, dog-like animal with strong jaws and a short, thick tail. Devils have black fur, often with white blazes around their necks and rump.

Average size and weight: Size varies depending on habitat, but head and body about 60cm, tail 24cm. Males weigh 5–13kg, females 4.5–9kg.

Behaviour: Nocturnal, they can travel 10–20km a night through their home range, sheltering during the day in grass-lined dens, hollow logs, caves or wombat burrows. They move clumsily, with a rocking horse-like gait, although young devils are agile enough to climb trees. They make a variety of sounds: snorts, low barks and growls, which turn into high-pitched screeching when fighting with other devils over food. When agitated or frightened their ears turn red.

Diet: Hunters and scavengers, they will eat just about anything of animal origin, including fur and bones, either cleaning up a carcass or killing wallabies, wombats, possums, small mammals and birds. Aluminium foil, steel pot scrapers, parts of leather boots and echidna quills have also been found in their droppings. Devils can feed on carrion in groups of up to 22, their voracious appetites meaning they can consume up to 40 per cent of their body weight in a single sitting.

Habitat: Found in all habitats, but prefers open forest, woodland and farmland.

Distribution: Found right across Tasmania. Died out on the mainland about 400 years ago, probably due to competition from the introduced dingo. In Tasmania the devil is now listed as endangered because of Devil Facial Tumour Disease.

photo: Dave Watts

Tasmanian pademelon (e)
Thylogale billardierii

Also known as rufous-bellied pademelons, rufous wallabies or red-bellied pademelons, these compact, short-tailed wallabies are common throughout Tasmania. They are often seen along the Overland, sometimes in conjunction with Bennett's wallabies, which are larger and have a black nose and paws. The unusual word pademelon is believed to be Aboriginal in origin. They make well-defined tracks through the bush as they move from their daytime resting areas to grassy areas to feed.

Description: Small and stocky, the Tasmanian pademelon has long, dark to golden brown fur and a red-brown belly. With its small size and short tail it's well adapted for moving through dense vegetation.

Average size and weight: Head and body 60cm, tail 40cm. Males average 7kg, females smaller and lighter.

Behaviour: Nocturnal animals, they sleep in dense, moist thickets during the day, emerging at dusk but rarely straying more than 100m from cover. During winter, or in bad weather, they might emerge earlier.

Diet: Herbs, leaves, green shoots and soft grasses, often eaten held in forepaws.

Habitat: Tea-tree scrub, woodland, temperate rainforest with dense undergrowth and near grassy areas.

Distribution: Once occurred on the mainland but now extinct due to foxes and land clearing. They remain common in Tasmania.

Bennett's wallaby
Macropus rufogriseus

photo: Dave Watts

Known as red-necked wallabies on the mainland, these large wallabies are often mistaken for kangaroos. The Bennett's wallabies that are common in Cradle Mountain–Lake St Clair National Park are the Tasmanian sub-species *Macropus rufogriseus subsp. rufogriseus*.

Description: Grey-brown on upper body, reddish brown on backs of ears, neck and shoulders (hence red-necked). Whiteish beneath. Can be distinguished from a pademelon by its black nose and paws. The Tasmanian variety has a shaggier coat to suit the cooler conditions.

Average size and weight: Head and body 80cm, tail about the same. Males average 15kg, females significantly smaller and lighter.

Behaviour: Spend the day resting in thick scrub, emerging in the late afternoon or evening to feed in open areas near forest shelter. Although they are solitary animals, they often congregate in mobs at feeding sites.

Diet: Grasses and herbs.

Habitat: Favour a mix of open grassy areas with nearby forest for shelter.

Distribution: The creation of farms and the reduction in hunting means the population has increased over the last 30 years. Found in coastal and highland areas through most of south-eastern Australia. Common.

Common wombat
Vombatus ursinus

photo: Dave Watts

Instantly loveable with their barrel-shaped body and characteristic waddle, most hikers will know wombats have been on the Overland from their brown cube-shaped droppings which are often left as scent markers on rocks or fallen branches.

Description: Solid, barrel-shaped body with small ears and eyes and a large flat nose. Their stiff, coarse fur varies from dull sandy-brown to blackish, paler beneath. Its short legs and large paws are adapted for digging.

Average size and weight: Tasmanian wombats are slightly smaller than those on the mainland, averaging 85cm in length and weighing up to 20kg.

Behaviour: Mostly nocturnal, they graze for 3–8 hours a night, travelling up to 3km and visiting several burrows in their home range. They also emerge to graze on cool or overcast days.

Diet: Herbivores, they graze on grasses, rushes, sedges, roots and tubers.

Habitat: Found in most vegetation, but prefer areas where the soil makes it easier to burrow, such as heathland, open woodland and coastal scrub.

Distribution: South-eastern Australia, common. There are two other species of wombat found on the mainland, the southern hairy-nosed wombat and the northern hairy-nosed wombat.

BIRDS

Tasmania has about 220 species of land birds, around 30 of which may be commonly found along the Overland. Of the 12 species found only in Tasmania, 11, such as the black currawong and yellow wattlebird, may be seen along the track. These endemic species are marked with an '(e)'. As with the plants and other animals, the birds are arranged from smallest to largest.

Tasmanian thornbill (e)

Acanthiza ewingii

photo: Alan Fletcher

Description: Small, active bird, warm brown to olive-brown above, reddish forehead, flanks pale olive-grey, white undertail feathers. Very similar to the brown thornbill but found in wetter habitats. 10cm.

Behaviour: Feeds on small insects on foliage, either in canopy or mid storey.

Call: Various, including sharp, melodic 'tszit, tszit'.

Habitat: Dense, damp areas in rainforest and wet eucalypt forest.

Distribution: Common.

photo: Alan Fletcher

Silvereye

Zosterops lateralis

Description: Colours vary. Head olive green, back blue-grey, throat and breast light grey and flanks chestnut to dull brown. As its common name implies, it has a conspicuous white eye-ring. 11cm.

Behaviour: Busy little birds, often seen feeding in flowering shrubs near the track. Also feed on fruit and insects. Many birds migrate to the mainland for winter.

Call: Alarm call, wavering 'weeee-ee-ee-ee', also calls continually while feeding, a thin, drawn-out 'psee'.

Habitat: Diverse: nearly anywhere with trees.

Distribution: Eastern and southern Australia. Also New Zealand, Pacific islands to Fuji. Common.

photo: Alan Fletcher

Pink robin

Petroica rodinogaster

Description: A quiet bird. Males: blackish above, belly rose pink. Females: overall fawny-brown. 12cm.

Behaviour: Waits patiently on a low perch then darts to the ground to snatch an insect.

Call: A sharp 'tick', also a soft warble.

Habitat: Dense, dark rainforest understorey. Moves to more open forest in autumn–winter.

Distribution: South-eastern Australia.

Tasmanian scrubwren (e)
Sericornis humilis

photo: Alan Fletcher

Description: Grey-brown to olive-brown above, with a fine white line above the eye, paler beneath. 13cm.

Behaviour: Shy, keeps near the ground where it feeds on insects among the leaf litter.

Call: Hikers are likely to hear its alarm call when it's disturbed near the track, a harsh rasping chatter.

Habitat: Dense thickets in woodland and rainforest.

Distribution: Common in Tasmania. Was previously considered the same species as the white-browed scrubwren on the mainland.

Black-headed honeyeater (e)
Melithreptus affinis

photo: Alan Fletcher

Description: Olive-brown, white below with a black hood over head and throat (no white band on back of neck). 14cm.

Behaviour: Feeds busily on insects on the leaves of middle and upper storey.

Call: Birds chatter as they feed, a high, sharp whistle 'tseip, tseip, tseip', also a harsh, rasping 'kherrk'.

Habitat: Forest and woodland. Avoids rainforest.

Distribution: Common.

Welcome swallow
Hirundo neoxena

photo: Alan Fletcher

Description: In summer welcome swallows are often seen in or near the nests they build under huts' eaves. Shiny-blue black, grey beneath with chestnut throat, face and forehead. Their tails deeply forked. 15cm.

Behaviour: Wheeling and swooping low to catch flying insects.

Call: A 'chep' in flight, also a cheery, twittering song.

Habitat: Diverse: avoids dense forest and desert.

Distribution: Across Australia, apart from the most arid regions. May migrate north from Tasmania in autumn–winter. Common.

Crescent honeyeater
Phylidonyris pyrrhopterus

photo: Alan Fletcher

Description: The most common honeyeater along the Overland, named after the thick black bands that run down either side of the bird's whiteish breast, almost meeting at the lower breast to form a crescent shape. Males: dark grey with thin white eyebrow, bright yellow panel on wing and long, curved bill. Females: duller with an indistinct 'crescent'. 16cm.

Behaviour: Busily forages for nectar and insects. Migrates to lower altitudes in winter.

Call: Loud, carrying 'eejik', also various melodic twitters.

Habitat: Diverse: woodlands, heathland, rainforest, but prefers thick scrub.

Distribution: South-eastern Australia. Common.

photo: Alan Fletcher

Strong-billed honeyeater (e)
Melithreptus validirostris

Description: Olive green, pale grey-brown beneath. Black cap with a white band running from behind the eyes across the back of neck. Large, straight beak. 17cm.

Behaviour: Hikers might hear this honeyeater as it energetically rips bark from tree trunks and branches with its powerful beak in search of ants, insects, spiders, bugs and beetles.

Call: Loud, sharp 'cheep, cheep'.

Habitat: Forest and heaths.

Distribution: Common.

photo: Alan Fletcher

New Holland honeyeater
Phylidonyris novaehollandiae

Description: Streaked black and white breast with yellow on wing and tail and a conspicuous white eye. With its long, slender beak and even longer tongue it's well adapted to probe flowers for nectar. 18cm.

Behaviour: Bold and restless, they dart from branch to branch searching for nectar and insects in flowering shrubs such as banksia, grevillea and waratah.

Call: A variety, but often draws attention with its loud, high-pitched alarm 'chweip-chwiep-chiwiep'.

Habitat: Eucalypt woodland with shrubby understorey, heaths and coastal thickets.

Distribution: Coastal south and east Australia. Common. The Tasmanian bird is considered a subspecies, *canescens*.

photo: Alan Fletcher

Yellow-throated honeyeater (e)
Lichenostomus flavicollis

Description: Upperparts olive green, grey/black head and breast, bright yellow throat. 20cm.

Behaviour: Noisy, bold, restlessly probing under loose bark for insects.

Call: Variety of calls including a musical whirring 'whit-chor, whit-chor' and a loud, metallic 'tonk-tonk-tonk'.

Habitat: Wide variety, particularly eucalypts, but not rainforest.

Distribution: Common.

photo: Alan Fletcher

Grey shrike-thrush
Colluricincla harmonica

Description: Olive-brown to grey, paler grey beneath. Unassuming to look at, this bird is renowned for its beautiful ringing calls, as indicated by its name *harmonica*. 24cm.

Behaviour: Forages on tree trunks, branches and on ground, often around fallen logs, its diet including insects, spiders, frogs and lizards.

Call: One of the better known Australian songbirds, with a variety of rich, ringing, melodic calls including a typical 'quorra-quorra-quorra, whieet-chiew'.

Habitat: Forest.

Distribution: Across Australia, apart from the most arid areas. Also southern New Guinea. The Tasmanian variety is considered a subspecies, *strigata*. Common.

Southern boobook

Ninox novaeseelandiae

photo: Alan Fletcher

Description: Australia's smallest and most common owl, also known as a mopoke. White-spotted dark-brown above, reddish brown mottled with white beneath. 25–36cm.

Behaviour: Nocturnal, it perches at dusk awaiting prey, taking moths and bats on the wing and mice and other small animals on the ground. Like all owls, its soft feathers mean it can fly silently, surprising its prey. During the day it roosts in dense foliage.

Call: Lying in a hut at night you're sure to hear its mournful cry, 'mo-poke'.

Habitat: Prefers open forest and woodland, but found nearly anywhere with trees.

Distribution: Across Australia. Also closely related species in New Zealand, New Guinea and Indonesia. The Tasmanian variety is considered a subspecies, *leucopsis*.

Green rosella (e)

Platycercus caledonicus

photo: Alan Fletcher

Description: The largest species of rosella, upperparts dark-green, greenish-yellow below with blue cheeks and red forehead. 32–38cm.

Behaviour: Feeds on ground or among tree foliage, eating seeds, fruit and berries.

Call: Shrill alarm calls, also three piercing whistles 'whee-whieit-whee'.

Habitat: Diverse: apart from treeless moorland and farmland.

Distribution: Common.

Yellow wattlebird (e)
Anthochaera paradoxa

photo: Alan Fletcher

Description: Australia's largest honeyeater is named for its distinctive yellow 'wattles' (long lobes that droop from each cheek). Feathers whiteish with dark streaks, yellow on belly. 38–48cm.

Behaviour: Gathers in flowering eucalypts and shrubs to feed on nectar and insects.

Call: Harsh, grating, guttural cough/vomit.

Habitat: Eucalypt forest, banksia woodland and heathland.

Distribution: Common.

Black currawong (e)
Strepera fuliginosa

photo: Alan Fletcher

Description: Black all over, apart from small white patches on wing and under tail. Large black bill and bright yellow eye. 45–50cm.

Behaviour: Forages in leaf litter and low vegetation for insects, grubs, lizards, mice and worms. Can occur in flocks of up to 50 in winter when they descend from the highlands to lower areas. Bold and intelligent they have learned to ransack unattended packs for food – even opening zips. The fruit-filled 'scats' along the track are actually the regurgitated remains of mountain pinkberries eaten by black currawongs.

Call: Loud, wheeling 'kar-week-week-kar'. Tasmanians associate the call with the highlands.

Habitat: Mainly subalpine forest and woodland.

Distribution: Common.

photo: Alan Fletcher

Tasmanian native hen (e)
Tribonyx mortierii

Description: One of only three flightless birds in Australia (along with the emu and cassowary), the Tasmanian native hen is distantly related to the domestic chicken. Olive-brown on top, slate grey beneath with a small whiteish patch on flank. Large yellow-green bill and bright red eye. 42–50cm.

Behaviour: Sometimes called turbo chickens, they can flee danger at up to 50km/h. Good swimmers. Often seen near dawn and dusk feeding on grasses and seeds.

Call: Noisy birds, often joining together in a loud, rasping 'see-saw' call.

Habitat: Open areas around swamps, marshes and lakes.

Distribution: Once found on the mainland, they became extinct about the time the dingo was introduced. Now found only in Tasmania, mostly in the north and east. Preyed upon by Tasmanian devils, quolls and birds of prey. Look for them near Waterfall Valley Huts, Lake Windermere, New Pelion Hut and Lake St Clair.

photo: Alan Fletcher

Forest raven
Corvus tasmanicus

Description: The largest species of raven and the only member of the crow family in Tasmania. Sleek and black with a large, powerful beak. It can be distinguished from the black currawong by its white eye. 53cm.

Behaviour: Often heard giving territorial call from high perch in tree. Appears in large flocks in winter. Feeds on carrion, grubs and berries.

Call: Deep, harsh 'karr, karr, kar-r- r–r', the last note drawn out and fading away.

Habitat: Diverse, widespread. Often seen beside roads eating carrion.

Distribution: Common in Tasmania, less common southern mainland range.

Yellow-tailed black cockatoo

Calyptorhynchus funereus

photo: Alan Fletcher

Description: A distinctive large black bird with yellow panel on tail and side of head. 58–65cm.

Behaviour: Can appear in pairs or large flocks, flying with slow, lazy wingbeats. Uses powerful beak to feed on seed capsules of banksias, hakeas and pines, the shredded remains often found on the track. Also chews into sapwood of wattles and sheoaks in search of grubs.

Call: Prehistoric, wailing 'weee-lah' and harsh alarm screeches.

Habitat: Forest, woodland and coastal heathland.

Distribution: Eastern and south-eastern Australia. Fairly common.

Wedge-tailed eagle

Aquila audax

photo: Alan Fletcher

Description: Australia's largest bird of prey, dark with a pale bill and a wing-span to 2.5m. Soaring high overhead it can be identified by its long, diamond-shaped tail. 75–85cm.

Behaviour: Usually seen soaring in large circles, alone or in pairs, or else perched in a dead tree with a commanding view. Feeds on rabbits, marsupials and carrion.

Call: Often silent, but sometimes a double high-pitched 'pee-yaa'.

Habitat: Hunts over open country but nests in woodland.

Distribution: Found all over Australia. The Tasmanian subspecies, *Aquila audax fleayi*, has evolved in isolation for 10,000 years and is listed as endangered with an estimated population of around 300 pairs. Hikers can sometimes see them soaring above Mt Pelion East. Shy nesters, logging threatens their survival, as does illegal shooting, electrocution on powerlines and poisoning.

SNAKES

White-lipped snake
Drysdalia coronoides

photo: Michael Thow

Description: Small, slender snake ranging in colour from dark olive green to a green-grey, light grey beneath. Also known as whip snakes, their common name 'white-lipped' comes from the stripe running from nostril to side of neck along upper lip. Young snakes have brightly coloured yellow-red bellies. Shy creatures, they have small fangs. In the unlikely event of being bitten they probably won't cause serious injury. They can be active in winter as their small size allows them to warm quickly.

Size: The smallest snake in Tasmania, around 50cm long.

Habitat: Feed primarily on small skinks in heaths, grasslands and woodlands.

Distribution: South-eastern Australia. The most cold-adapted snake in Australia. Preyed upon by the kookaburra, an introduced species to Tasmania.

Lowland copperhead
Austrelaps superbus

photo: Michael Thow

Description: Variable in colour, copperheads range from black through coppery brown to a dull brick red. Most adults have an orange-brown stripe running horizontally above their cream-yellow belly. Compared to a tiger snake its head is relatively narrow, about as broad as its body. They are placid, but dangerously venomous.

Size: 1–1.3m.

Habitat: Near marshes, swamps and streams under 1000m. They feed mainly upon frogs and lizards, although they also eat smaller snakes – including other copperheads.

Distribution: Drier parts of Tasmania and southern Victoria.

Tiger snake
Notechis scutatus

photo: Michael Thow

Description: Highly variable in colour, tiger snakes range from black to grey or even yellow. Despite the name 'tiger' they may or may not have bands around their body. The belly is generally a pale yellow or grey. They are difficult to tell apart from copperheads. Dangerously venomous.

Although the Tasmanian tiger snake is often darker than those occurring on southern mainland Australia, they are the same species.

Size: 1–1.5m.

Habitat: Most, including grassland, woodlands and dry rocky areas. They are particularly abundant around wet marshes where there are plenty of frogs to eat. They also eat small mammals, birds, lizards and skinks.

Distribution: Although the Tasmanian tiger snake is often darker than those occurring on southern mainland Australia, they are the same species.

APPENDIX A

Useful contacts

Australia's international telephone prefix is +61.

Emergency services

Police, fire and ambulance
tel 000

Accommodation

Cradle Valley

Cradle Mountain Highlanders
3876 Cradle Mountain Road
Cradle Mountain
tel 03 6492 1116
www.cradlehighlander.com.au

Cradle Mountain Hotel
3718 Cradle Mountain Rd
Cradle Mountain
tel 03 6492 1404
www.cradlemountainhotel.com.au

Cradle Mountain Lodge
4038 Cradle Mountain Rd
Cradle Mountain
tel 03 6492 2100
www.cradlemountainlodge.com.au

Cradle Mountain Wilderness Village
3816 Cradle Mountain Road
Cradle Mountain
tel 03 6492 1500
www.cradlevillage.com.au

Discovery Parks Cradle Mountain
3832 Cradle Mountain Road
Cradle Mountain
tel 03 6492 1395
www.discoveryholidayparks.com.au

Waldheim Cabins
Connells Avenue
Cradle Mountain
tel 03 6491 2158
www.cradleinfo.com.au

Cynthia Bay and Derwent River

Derwent Bridge Chalets and Studios
15478 Lyell Highway
Derwent Bridge
tel 03 6289 1000
www.derwent-bridge.com

Derwent Bridge Wilderness Hotel
15573 Lyell Hwy
Derwent Bridge
tel 03 6289 1144
www.derwentbridgewildernesshotel.com.au

Lake St Clair Lodge
Lake St Clair Road
Lake St Clair
tel 03 6289 1137
www.lakestclairlodge.com.au

Pumphouse Point
1 Lake St Clair Road
Lake St Clair
tel 0428 090 436
www.pumphousepoint.com.au

Information

Bureau of Meteorology
www.bom.gov.au

Cradle Mountain Visitor Centre
tel 03 6492 1110

Lake St Clair Visitor Centre
tel 03 6289 1172

Overland Track Booking Service &
Overland Track Administrator
tel 03 6165 4254
www.overlandtrack.com.au

Tasmania Parks and Wildlife Service
tel 1300 827 727
www.parks.tas.gov.au

Save the Tasmanian Devil Program
www.tassiedevil.com.au

Tasmanian wilderness conservation information
www.wilderness.org.au

Other

devils@cradle
(Tasmanian devil sanctuary)
3950 Cradle Mountain Rd
Cradle Mountain
tel 03 6492 1491
www.devilsatcradle.com

Hungry Wombat Café
15488 Lyell Hwy
Derwent Bridge
tel 03 6289 1125

The Wall in the Wilderness
15352 Lyell Hwy
Derwent Bridge
tel 03 6289 1134
www.thewalltasmania.com.au

Visa information
www.homeaffairs.gov.au

Overland Track tour companies

Cradle Mountain Huts Walk
tel 03 6392 2211
www.taswalkingco.com.au

Tasmanian Expeditions
tel 1300 666 856
www.tasmanianexpeditions.com.au

Tasmanian Hikes
tel 0400 882 742
www.tasmanianhikes.com.au

Tasmanian Photography Workshops
tel 0413 487 644
www.camblakephotography.com.au

Tasmanian Wilderness Experiences
tel 0477 480 383
www.twe.travel

Trek Tasmania
tel 1300 133 278
www.trektasmania.com.au

Wilderness Expeditions Tasmania
tel 0499 660 120
www.wildernessexpeditions.net.au

Transport

Bus companies with scheduled services

McDermott's Coaches
tel 03 6330 3717
www.mcdermotts.com.au

Overland Track Transport
tel 0474 172 012
www.overlandtracktransport.com.au

Chartered buses

Cradle Mountain Coaches
tel 03 6427 7626
www.cradlemountaincoaches.com.au

Outdoor Tasmania
tel 0408 918 249
www.outdoortasmania.com.au

Overland Track Transport
tel 0474 172 012
www.overlandtracktransport.com.au

Tasmanian Road Trips
tel 0455 227 536
www.tassieroadtrips.com

Transport Tasmania (Tasmanian Wilderness Experiences)
tel 0477 480 383
www.twe.travel

Air

Jetstar Airways
tel 131 538
www.jetstar.com

Qantas & Qantas Linktel 131 313
www.qantas.com.au

Tigerair
tel 1300 174 266
www.tigerair.com.au

Virgin Australia
tel 136 789
www.virginblue.com.au

Ferry

Lake St Clair ferry (Ida Clair)
tel 03 6289 1137
www.lakestclairlodge.com.au

Spirit of Tasmania Ferry
tel 1800 634 906
www.spiritoftasmania.com.au

APPENDIX B

Suggested clothing, gear and food

SUGGESTED CLOTHING LIST

- Hooded, breathable waterproof jacket. This will keep out the wind and rain; thigh-length will keep you drier.
- Waterproof over-pants. Although they can be constricting to walk in, if the weather turns bad they're invaluable. As with the jacket, breathable ones are best. They can also be worn when walking through prickly vegetation.
- Sturdy hiking boots, in good condition and with good soles and ankle support, as much of the Overland is over rough, uneven ground. Make sure they're worn in before you hit the track to avoid blisters.
- Good quality hiking socks. Make sure they have no seams in places likely to cause blisters.
- Underwear.
- Synthetic or fine merino T-shirt.
- Thermal pants and thermal top. Can be the base layer worn against the skin. In cold weather these will be your new best friends. Polypropylene thermals are effective and reasonably priced but, if you can afford them, Icebreaker or similar merino-wool thermals work over a wider range of temperatures, stay comfortable and resist getting stinky.
- Shorts.
- Collapsible broad-brimmed sunhat.
- Gloves (or else you might be finding another use for your socks).
- Beanie.
- Warm top. The insulating layer, a long-sleeved fleece or woollen jumper.
- A light, long-sleeved shirt with collar for sun protection.
- Loose, comfortable pants.
- Sunglasses.
- Small towel or face washer.
- A complete set of camp clothes – pants, socks and top – so you always have something dry to change into at the end of a day's walk.
- Many hikers would also add gaiters to this list to protect their lower legs when ploughing through prickly vegetation, deep mud or snow. They also offer some protection in the unlikely event of a snakebite.
- In cold weather an extra warm layer, such as a vest, should be considered.

SUGGESTED GEAR LIST

- Backpack. Backpacks have the amazing ability to always be full, so resist the temptation to buy the largest available. For a multi-day hike such as the Overland, a pack with a 55–75 litre capacity should be sufficient; the exact size depends on whether you're walking alone or as part of a group (where there are more people to carry the gear). Make sure your pack is large enough to carry your tent and sleeping bag inside the pack – having large items tied to the outside of your pack isn't ergonomic and the items are likely to get torn and wet. Some things to look for in a pack include suitable harness length, an effective waist-belt, tough material, good stitching, sturdy zips and convenient pockets and straps.

- Daypack. If you're planning to do any of the sidetrips then bring a small, collapsible daypack. A daypack allows you to ditch your main pack at a sidetrip junction or hut, while still allowing you to take necessities and keep your hands free for climbing.
- First aid kit. My suggested basic first aid kit has two 10cm-wide pressure bandages for snakebite, strains or fractures; antiseptic for minor cuts and burns; six Band-aids; tweezers; antihistamines for insect bites; four blister pads; Gastro-stop (or similar); roll of adhesive tape for preventing blisters such as Leukoplast or similar zinc oxide tape; Nurofen pain killers (or similar); two sets of three wound-closure strips; absorbent non-adherent dressing (to stop dressing sticking to wound) and a survival blanket.
- Sunscreen.
- Pack cover to help keep the worst of the rain off your pack and to protect it from animals while on sidetrips.
- Insect repellent.
- Fuel stove and fuel. The national park is a fuel-stove-only area. There is no cooking equipment in any of the huts.
- Knife, fork and/or spoon. There are lots of lightweight hiking models available.
- Mug and a plate that doubles as a bowl.
- Roll mat. Slim inflatable ones such as Therm-a-Rest brand are the best as they're small, comfortable and conserve body heat. There are no mattresses in the huts.
- Comfortable camp shoes such as sandals, flip flops or Crocs.
- Sleeping bag (rated to -5°C or lower).
- Sleeping bag liner to keep your sleeping bag clean.
- A tough bin bag to line the inside of your pack. The Cradle Mountain and Lake St Clair visitor centres sell pack-liners. While a pack cover helps keep your pack dry, adding a pack-liner ensures it.
- Earplugs. Huts are small and snorers are loud.

- Plastic bags to carry out your litter. Also take spare bags of various sizes, including zip-locks, which are useful for keeping things dry or isolating dirty gear.
- LED headtorch.
- Small trowel (in case you need to dig a bush toilet).
- Toilet paper (there's none provided on the track).
- Toiletries, including liquid hand-sanitiser.
- Tent. Even if you are planning to sleep in the huts, bringing a small tent is strongly recommended. Huts are sometimes crowded and noisy and in an emergency a tent could save your life.
- Some lengths of string or cord allow for flexibility when attaching your tent to the camping platform cables. String is also handy for hanging food bags from hut rafters: essential for keeping them out of the reach of mice and possums.
- Cigarette lighter and waterproof matches.
- Swiss army knife or similar (they're just bloody handy).
- 1.5 litre drink bottle (or larger), or a CamelBak-type water dispenser.
- A collapsible 2-litre water bladder for storing water while at huts.
- Camera/mobile phone – phone apps such as MAPS.ME provide free off-line maps; an invaluable back-up to an old-school paper map.
- Small repair kit with needle and thread. You can get ones the size of a matchbox for a couple of dollars.
- Map – Tasmap's Cradle Mountain–Lake St Clair 1:100,000.
- GPS/compass. Especially for sidetrips like The Labyrinth.
- Pot scourer. With a good scourer you won't need detergent.
- Whistle. To attract attention in case of emergency.
- A novelty or two in case you're hut-bound by bad weather – a book, pen and paper, crosswords, knitting...

Some other suggestions include sturdy cloth food bags, hiking poles, playing cards and a Personal Locator Beacon.

SUGGESTED FOOD LIST

Breakfast

Something that will stick to your ribs and power you until lunch.

- Porridge. Great energy value for weight. Can be jazzed up with sugar or dried fruit.
- Muesli, as above.
- Milk powder to make the above palatable and to add to tea and coffee.
- Tea bags, instant coffee (or coffee bags for a bit more flavour) and sugar.

Lunch

It's best to keep things simple and avoid heating anything up.

- Mountain Bread is a thin, flexible bread that's great for sandwiches or wraps (and also good as a naan-type bread for dinners). Many other pita bread-like products are also available.
- Rice Thins, Vita-Weats or similar crispbreads are also handy, but harder to avoid crushing.
- Popular toppings for the above include tuna (seek brands that come in sachets not cans), peanut butter, cheese and salami (but generally not all at the same time).

Dinner

After hiking all day don't disappoint yourself – get something tasty and substantial. 'Instant' just-add-hot-water hiking meals are widely available from outdoors shops, and although pricy for the relatively small serving sizes, they're light and easy to prepare. Packet soups can be a great starter to warm you up. Quick-cook rice can save time and fuel. Some hikers use home dehydrators to dry all their dinners before they go, even preparing extra for lunch the next day.

- Pasta, quick-cook rice, dhal, couscous or noodle-based meals are satisfying.
- Instant mashed potato is light and filling and can be a good accompaniment to other fare.
- Dehydrated foods are available in most supermarkets and make a good addition to dinners. These include mushrooms, beef jerky, peas, corn, onion, garlic and vegetables.
- Soup powder or stock cubes can add flavour to pasta or rice meals.
- Spices give any meal a lift – take small zip-lock bags of your favourites.

Snacks and treats

You'll be expending a lot of energy so make sure you carry plenty of snacks to power you up those hills.

- Nuts, dried fruit and muesli bars can provide a substantial boost when on the track.
- Trail mix or 'Scroggin', is a mix of dried fruit, nuts and sometimes chocolate that's popular with hikers.
- A chocolate bar or two.
- A hot chocolate in the evening can really hit the spot.

APPENDIX C

What now? Other hikes in Tasmania

There are enough hikes in Tassie to wear your legs to stubs. Here are just a few:

THE FREYCINET PENINSULA CIRCUIT

A 2–3 day, 30km hike looping through Freycinet National Park on the east coast of Tasmania. The walk traverses the beautiful Wineglass Bay, famous from a million postcards, and includes an optional climb to the top of Mount Freycinet (620m). For more information see www.parks.tas.gov.au.

THE THREE CAPES TRACK

Easy 4-day, 48km walk along the huge coastal cliffs of the Tasman National Park in south-east Tasmania sleeping in well-appointed huts. Bookings required. Visit www.threecapestrack.com.au for more information.

THE WALLS OF JERUSALEM CIRCUIT HIKE

Located in the national park of the same name, the Walls of Jerusalem borders the east side of the Cradle Mountain–Lake St Clair National Park and offers a 2–3 day, 34km circuit along a wild, remote plateau of tarns and pencil pine forest. For more information see www.trailhiking.com.au.

FRENCHMANS CAP

A tough 3–5 day, 47km hike to the top of one of the state's most distinctive peaks. The hike has two parts, first across boardwalks over the Loddon Plains and then into the mountains that rise steeply to the 1446m summit. The start of the walk is 28km west of Derwent Bridge. For more information visit www.parks.tas.gov.au.

THE SOUTH COAST TRACK

Hikers are flown to the start of the walk at Melaleuca via light plane – the only way out is to walk 85km east for 6 to 8 days, crossing beaches, rivers, headlands and buttongrass plains before reaching the road at Cockle Creek. For more information see www.southcoasttrack.com.au.

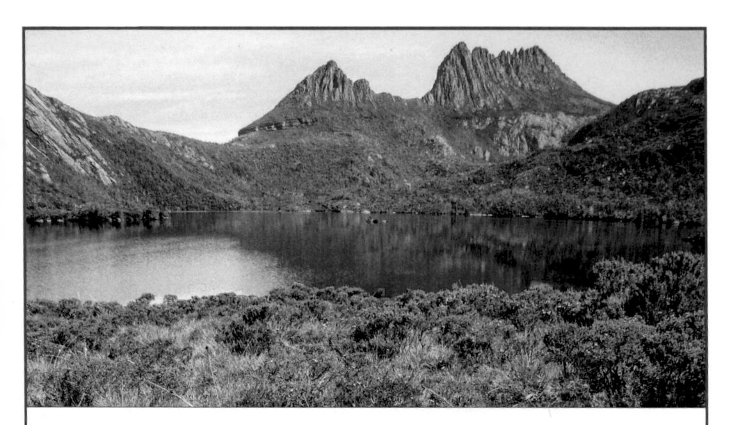

DOWNLOAD THE ROUTES IN GPX FORMAT

All the routes in this guide are available for download from:

www.cicerone.co.uk/1013/GPX

as GPX files. You should be able to load them into most formats of mobile device, whether GPS or smartphone.

When you go to this link, you will be asked for your email address and where you purchased the guide, and have the option to subscribe to the Cicerone e-newsletter.

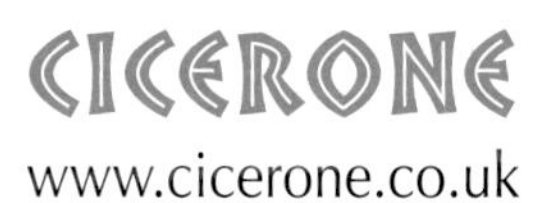

www.cicerone.co.uk

IF YOU ENJOYED THIS GUIDEBOOK YOU MIGHT ALSO BE INTERESTED IN...

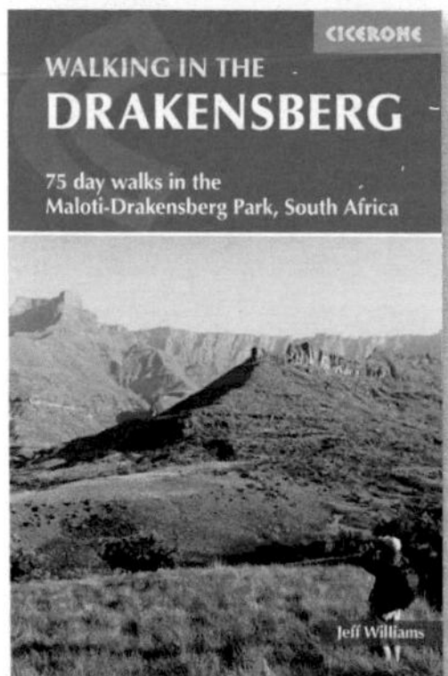

visit **www.cicerone.co.uk** for more detail and our full range of guidebooks